Lucille

AFGHANISTAN

T I B E T

KANDAHAR●

●LAHORE

IRAN

NEW DELHI ●

NEPAL

AGRA ●

BHUTAN

●KARACHI

ALLAHABAD●

ASANSOL●
BARRACKPORE

A S

CHAKULIA● ●DUM DUM
CALCUTTA●

I N D I A

AK

●BOMBAY

ARABIAN SEA

Bay of Bengal

ANDAMAN

BANGALORE●   ●MADRAS

ISLAND

N

●COCHIN

CEYLON

I N D I A N   O C E A N

FANITA
LANIER
1967

0   100   200 300 400 500

SCALE OF MILES

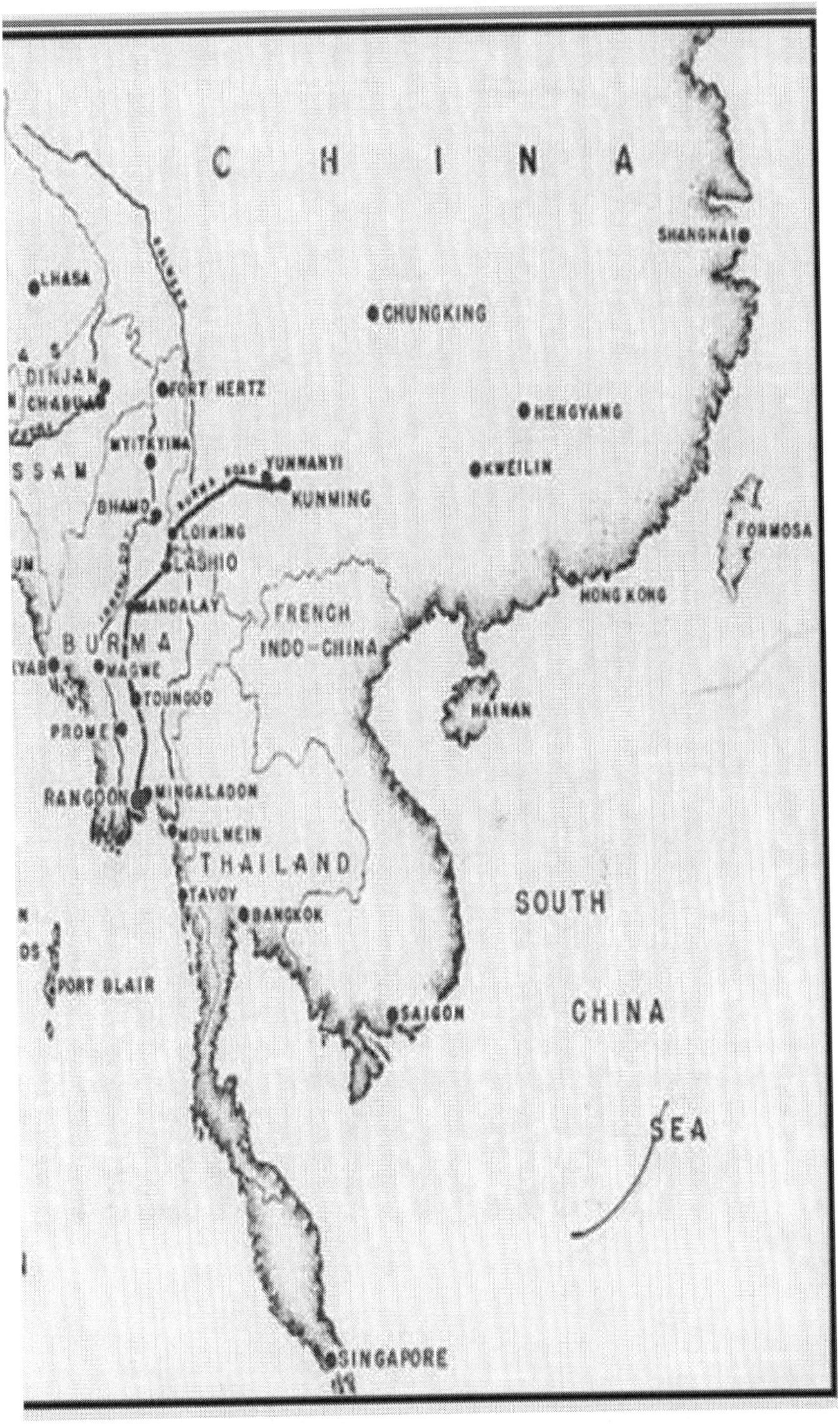

CHINA

SHANGHAI

LHASA

CHUNGKING

A S
DINJAN
N CHABUA

FORT HERTZ

HENGYANG

SSAM

MYITKYINA

YUNNANYI

KWEILIN

DHAMO

KUNMING

LOIWING

LASHIO

FORMOSA

MANDALAY

FRENCH
INDO-CHINA

HONG KONG

BURMA

YAB

MAGWE

TOUNGOO

HAINAN

PROME

RANGOON

MINGALADON

MOULMEIN

THAILAND

SOUTH

TAVOY

BANGKOK

CHINA

PORT BLAIR

SAIGON

SEA

SINGAPORE

This book is a true story.

Only certain names have been changed to protect the identities
of men who lost their lives in horrific ways as an effort to spare
their families this knowledge. Any resemblance to actual
persons, living or dead, is entirely coincidental.

Self published by Kenneth Horner

First published in trade paperback edition April 2013
First eBook published for Kindle® October 2013

Printed by CreateSpace ®
an Amazon.com Company ®
and

Manufactured in the United States of America

ISBN-13: 978-0615734026 (Custom)
ISBN-10: 0615734022

MISSING IN ACTION

Thirty-five months of survival as a guest of Emperor Hirohito

A MEMOIR

by

KENNETH "JACK" HORNER

DEDICATION

War should only be embarked
upon as an absolute last resort.
But once that line is crossed
and you find yourself in defense
of your homeland, know, that
you will be in the company
of the finest and the bravest.

So it was for me.

I was privileged to meet men
I would never have known
had it not been for the events
of the war that threw us together.

I dedicate this memoir to those
with whom I served, those with
whom I was imprisoned,
the ones that didn't make it home,
the one's that serve today and
all those who will serve tomorrow.

1 THE MISSION

During World War II, I was missing in action for 35 months, captured 600 miles behind enemy lines in the China Burma India Theater of Operations.

On my last day of freedom, June 3, 1942, I remember thinking "This is the way to fight a war!"

After ferrying our B-17 from Tampa, Florida we landed, on April 10, in the city of Karachi, India. (Pakistan and Bangladesh did not exist until after the end of World War II. They were created by the British to separate the Muslims from the Hindus). An air field had been established by the Army and for a few days we lived in tents because the number of airmen arriving far exceeded the capacity of the airdrome's dormitories. The food, as always, was American, well prepared, and delicious. We had bacon and eggs for breakfast, steak and potato for lunch and ice cream whenever we wanted it.

The Allies in the China Burma India Theater of Operation were the Chinese, under Chiang Kai-shek, who were fighting the Japanese in Southwest China, Great Britain and the United States. The Chinese Nationalist had also sent their Fifth and Sixth Armies South over the Burma Road to help defend Burma.

British forces with the help of Col. Claire Chennault's American Volunteer Group (Flying Tigers) defended Rangoon, but were unsuccessful. Rangoon was the end of the 700 mile long Burma Road and the only route by which to deliver war supplies to Chiang Kai-shek in China. The city was occupied by the Japanese on March 8, 1942, about one month before I arrived in India. An American, General "Vinegar Joe" Stillwell, was the supreme commander of the Allied forces.

On April 20 some of the planes from the Doolittle raid on Tokyo landed in Karachi. I did not have a chance to meet any of the airmen but they certainly were a heroic group. The raid was done by 16 B-25's, each with a crew of five. The raid was possible because the Hornet, an aircraft carrier, had taken the Air Force planes close enough to bomb Tokyo and then escape to China. I learned that we lost 14 of the 80 crew members.

In early May we were ordered to an airfield 1400 miles from Karachi, located in the desert city of Hyderabad. This became our home base for launching bombing raids. It was very much like an American airfield in every way. The only downside was that we were required to wear pith helmets because the temperature occasionally reached 120°. According to my service record I flew four reconnaissance and five combat missions.

One of the reconnaissance missions was to try to locate General "Vinegar Joe" Stillwell. As the British retreated on the Burma Road, General Stillwell decided that the

Japanese, who now were attacking with a three pronged offense, could be stopped at Mandalay and Rangoon retaken in a counter attack. His headquarters were located at Lasad and Myitkyina. When the Allies were defeated, the Chinese under his command retreated so rapidly that they overran his headquarters and there were only a few miles of road between him and the Japanese. He evacuated some of his staff from Myitkyina by plane. The remaining members, including doctors and nurses, boarded a train which had to be abandoned when they were stopped by an impassible barrier of bombed trains and track.

The escape group had grown to 141 staff, nurses, doctors and soldiers. They left the train with Jeeps and trucks to try to reach Imphal, India. Our mission was to locate them so that supplies could be dropped. Despite our failure to find them, the group was found and supported by air. General Stillwell reached safe haven without losing a person. During the 12 days that it took the General to reach Imphal, the Japanese had occupied the airdrome at Myitkyina. They were providing air support for troops attacking Imphal, India. On our first combat mission, five days after we searched for General Stillwell, we bombed the airdrome at Myitkyina.

The squadron did not lose any planes due to enemy action, however the crew of one plane was killed when the plane crashed while taking off. Other than the inherent danger of flying and the few moments they are exposed to combat, airmen enjoy a very comfortable life.

Date May 13, 1942, New Orleans, Louisiana.

ican Bombers in India
ag 75 Jap Planes in 8 Raids

Only One Machine—
That Through Ac-
cident During Takeoff

In India

By Preston Grover
(Wide World)

With the U. S. Bomber Command in India, May 13.—In their first eight moonlight raids Major General Lewis H. Brereton's U. S. Army bombers destroyed or damaged about 75 Japanese planes, messed up docks and shipping at Rangoon, and showered explosives on a Japanese fleet in the Andaman Islands, in the Bay of Bengal.

During that time they lost only one plane, and that through a take-off accident rather than by enemy action.

That is a short history of a bomber command operating 10,000 miles from home, from a base which must go without identification until the Japanese learn where it is. It's enough to say that these men are stationed in the most distant place from which an American bomber command ever has operated.

They are clear around on the other side of the world from America, and if the bombs they drop on Burma were to land in the corresponding latitude on the other side they'd make a mess out of Florida.

Planes Flown from U. S.

Every one of the planes now in service against the Japanese was flown here from the United States. They came across the Atlantic, on across Africa, and then to India. From here they fly 600 to 800 miles farther to attack enemy-held targets in Burma. Moreover, they'll be ready when the time comes to attack the Japanese launching a drive against India.

I flew from New Delhi to visit the bomber command as the first correspondent to see them actually at work. And they really have to work, despite heat which sometimes rises to 120 degrees and doesn't get below 100 for nights on end.

When I landed at the field, big four-motored Flying Fortresses were being loaded for a night attack. "Just in case" the Japanese should find the place, the bombers were dispersed over the field while each plane took on tons of gasoline and tons of bombs.

Maintenance crews kept testing and adjusting the planes to the last minute, though the afternoon sun had made the metal so hot it blistered their hands. For the widest possible margin of safety ground crews crowded in every last gallon of gasoline and every last pint of oil.

the great gray bulks too

SECOND LIEUTENANT KENNETH F. HORNER, American bombardier stationed at the Indian airdrome of the United States Army ferry command, is one of numerous Southerners serving with American forces in Indian stations, it was revealed Wednesday.

pancakes and syrup for breakfast. That's here. This probably also is the only place in India where you're likely to find apple pie on the menu.

Despite the heat and the fact their base is located in the midst of a scorched plain that is just as flat and as jungle-free as Kansas, the morale of this outfit is high.

If they do complain, it's only about the heat, about the holy cattle which get in front of their jeeps—and about the poor mail service. Most haven't had a letter since they got here months ago, but all are looking forward to the day when mail, now believed held up in Australia, finally gets through.

My father shows my mother my picture in the paper and an article about my group of planes bombing Myitkyna in Burma.

My father assures my mother that the B-17 was capable of flying high and out of reach of "ack-ack."

He had read about the accuracy of the Norden bombsight and he explained to my mother that it enabled the bombers to hit targets from very high altitudes where it would be difficult for the Zeros to operate.

He concludes that the Allies have been defeated in Burma and have retreated to India. He reads that in the South Pacific Ocean, six months after Pearl Harbor, we have enjoyed our first success. In the Battle of the Coral Sea, a combined American and Australian Naval Force defeated the Japanese and kept them from landing at Port Moresby, New Guinea.

2   THE BATTLE

I had participated in three night raids over Rangoon, Burma in our B-17. The conquering Japanese forces had installed many search lights and anti-aircraft guns in the city. A typical mission consisted of six or seven planes flying 900 miles from our home base in Hyderabad to be refueled at the staging area in Calcutta. We then flew in echelon 700 miles and dropped our bombs on the city because on night raids there was never a specific target. After a few moments of excitement when the search lights illuminated the planes we returned to our home base. Although no planes had been shot down, there was always some minor damage to some of the planes and one man had been killed by shrapnel. A raid on Rangoon took about 10 hours and we flew 3,000 miles.

A B-17 is staffed by four officers and five enlisted personnel. The officers are the pilot, copilot, navigator and bombardier. The enlisted personnel are the crew chief, who operates the top turret, and four personnel who man the bottom turret, the tail gun and the waist guns. The only other weapon is a .30 caliber machine gun, which could be moved from port to port by the navigator. The job of the pilot and copilot are, of course, to fly and steer the plane using compass headings they receive from the navigator. The navigator determines the proper course by using celestial observations and dead reckoning which is a method of calculating the position of the plane using speed, wind drift and elapsed time. The bombardier, with the help of the newest military technology, the Norden bombsight, controls when the bombs must be dropped to strike the target.

I was the navigator. The pilot was Capt. Douglas Sharp, an excellent pilot and a superb officer, the epitome of what a soldier should be.

Our new mission was to fly 3 planes, in daylight, to bomb Mingaladon airfield in Rangoon. It occurred to me that the daylight raid would be a little more dangerous than the night raid's. We had arrived the night before and were bivouacked in the finest hotel in Calcutta. The evening meal was terrific and it seemed there was a server for each diner. In the morning I was awakened in my room at the specified time with a "chute hare," which is a small breakfast of fruit and toast. Then, before we went to the airport for briefing, we had an unbelievably sumptuous breakfast.

My day started to sour a little when we found out that one plane was unable to make the mission. We were glad to learn, however, that, according to intelligence, we would not encounter any Japanese fighter planes (Zeros).

On the way to Rangoon, about one hour into the flight, my day soured a little more when we learned the second plane had to abort the flight. From my training

I knew that three planes can create a pretty formidable defense against enemy fighters and that losing two planes greatly increased the vulnerability of our plane. There was no discussion amongst us, yet I'm sure everyone realized the increased danger. I think we all took some comfort from the fact that, according to intelligence, there were no enemy aircraft protecting Rangoon. I may have been simply naïve but I never felt threatened or frightened. My main concern was that I would conduct myself properly if engaged in combat.

I mentioned Capt. Douglas Sharp earlier because, in my opinion, he was the perfect soldier. As we approached the target, Lt. George Wilson, the bombardier, reported that there was cloud cover and he could not use his bomb-sight.

Doug to George, very calmly,"The port is clear. When I get it lined up, pick a ship."

The plane was at 10,000 feet. Even though there were clouds above us, we could see shipping in the port. We had to make a 180 degree turn to get lined up on the target. It seemed to take forever to make the turn.

Top turret reports a Zero to everyone over the intercom "Bandit! At two o'clock high!"

We're now in the bomb run and Doug cannot maneuver the plane defensively. I felt the twin 50s as the tail gunner began firing and moments thereafter I heard the top turret and the waist gun.

George shouted "Bombs away."

Doug immediately turned towards an incoming Zero to make him tighten up his dive.

Doug to me, "Jack, there is a plane at 10 o'clock high. Here he comes."

I started firing the .30 caliber. The .30 caliber has tracer bullets so that you can see where the bullets are going. I was not certain whether or not I hit the Zero, but I knew he hit us. The bullet came through the front compartment between George and me. After the bombs dropped we were engaged in a battle against 24 Zeros for over 20 minutes as Doug tried to reach cloud cover. As we approached the clouds, I knew we had been hit at least three times and that the waist gunner, a young private, Francis Tehan, had been killed. I was also pretty certain that we had shot down four or five Zeros. The top and bottom turrets no longer operated. My gun was jammed and only the tail guns were still operating. We were in no position to defend ourselves when we entered the clouds.

George and I heard the alarm which meant prepare to jump. Neither George nor I were wearing parachutes during the combat but after my gun jammed I had turned my attention to them rather frantically because I realized the bullets through our compartment could have hit the parachutes and made them useless. After a quick examination we put on the parachutes and waited for the signal to jump. Even though I could not communicate with Capt. Sharp, I remembered the many times I expressed a desire to stay with the plane if it was possible. I heard the signal and jumped from the plane about three o'clock in the afternoon.

I pulled the rip cord and the parachute opened perfectly.

3 THE WELCOME

As I drifted slowly down to earth, I realized I had no knowledge that would help me when I encountered natives of Burma. I knew that in Europe an underground system had been established to help airmen to escape capture and return to England or Portugal, a country that had remained neutral. I also realized that such a system did not exist in Burma. The only instruction I had been given officially was that if I was ever captured by the Japanese I had only to give, according to the Geneva Convention, my name, rank and serial number. I realized that without the help of the Burmese there would be little chance of negotiating 600 miles of swamp, forest and mountains to reach Allied troops.

As I got closer to the ground, I could see that I was going to land in the crescent of a river about 300 feet from a group of buildings. I landed on my feet in waist high grass. When I jumped, I was wearing a belt and holster with a .45

caliber pistol. I now found I had the belt and an empty holster. I had lost the pistol. While I was momentarily distressed for having lost the gun, I quickly realized it was of no consequence, as I was not in a position to use a gun to win safe passage back to the front lines. I had opened the backpack of the parachute and was picking out items I thought might be useful no matter what occurred. I lifted my head above the grass and saw that I was surrounded by seven or eight Burmese men armed with machetes.

I stood up and raised my right hand in what I hoped was the universal sign for peace. It certainly worked in the movies I had seen. After a moment, I raised my left hand to show that I had no weapon. The men converged on my position in a way that appeared to be non-threatening and even peaceful. As they got near I asked if anyone spoke English. The chatter between them indicated they did not.

By sign language they told me to go towards the village I had seen from the air. We emerged from the grass and after about 100 feet I was escorted into a bungalow. I immediately asked an elderly man who was seated on the floor. "Do you speak English?"

He seemed to understand what I asked him and shook his head in the negative. There were two women present and one indicated by sign language that she wanted to dry my clothes. While I had no intention of taking off my clothes, I was very anxious to have them get a favorable opinion of me and, therefore, I took off and gave her my shirt. I probably would not be alive today were it not for that insignificant gesture. The second woman offered me a small plate full of sliced mango. Although mangos are plentiful, this was to be the last piece of fruit I ate in Burma.

The old man offered me a Sears Roebuck catalog, which I accepted hoping that I could somehow use it to communicate with him. I was on my knees in front of him, racking my brain for a way to communicate that I needed someone who could help me avoid being captured by the Japanese.

I felt reasonably safe and in no hurry to embark without some direction. I noticed suddenly that his eyes, which had been focused on me, were now looking above my head. I turned to see two young Burmese men pointing single barrel shotguns at me. I looked back at the elderly fellow and he said in excellent English, "These are the Burmese Home Guard."

I remember saying, "You speak English."

He said, "Yes my son."

The Home Guard did not have uniforms, but they did have guns, which automatically gave them a hell of a lot of authority. They motioned me outside and walked me in the direction of the field that I crossed to reach the old man's bungalow. After 30 or 40 yards, they stopped at the edge of the open field. They then turned me around so that I was facing the bungalow.

While one of them pointed the shotgun at me, the other moved behind my back and removed my wallet from my pocket and my chronometer from my wrist. As they tied my hands behind my back I realized they intended to execute me. The old man had followed us from the house and a good sized crowd had gathered to watch the execution. I experienced what I think is called an "out of body" vision. I saw myself dead, lying on the ground and the people moving in to look at me.

I can't imagine what possessed me to do it, but I started shouting that I was an American officer and not a spy and I wanted to be in my uniform if I was going to be shot. The old man translated what I said and someone was sent to retrieve my shirt. When the shirt was brought, my hands were untied and I was permitted to put it on. I unbuckled my belt and trousers so I could tuck the tail into my pants. My hands were again tied behind my back and one of the execution pair tried to put a blindfold over my eyes. I shook my head to show that I didn't want it.

At that precise moment, I saw some sort of activity at the edge of the river. One of the self-appointed firing - squad held a gun on me while the other insisted that he be allowed to tie on a blindfold. From the confusion at the river's edge, a man came running to where I stood with the two executioners. He was evidently a person of authority.

After talking to the firing squad he addressed me in somewhat broken and singsong English, "I am the Japanese representative in this area. These young men want to kill you, but I must take you to the Japanese. They will want to question you and then they will kill you."

I remember saying something silly like, "You are doing the right thing because the Japanese will certainly want to talk to me."

The four of us began walking while my hands were still tied behind my back. They weren't tied very well and no one noticed when I untied my hands and dropped the rope. After two hours we entered a building where I spent the night. The accommodations were considerably different from the ones I had enjoyed 24 hours earlier.

My captors were seated at a table talking to each other and appeared to be unaware of my presence until I asked for a drink of water. The Japanese representative brought me the water and, pointing to the corner of the room, told me that was where I could sleep. When I woke up I saw that the Japanese representative was alone at the table. I indicated I needed to urinate and a shout from him brought in two uniformed policeman with rifles. One of them escorted me to a well-appointed bathroom.

When we returned, the representative invited me to eat some cereal and milk which were on the table. He became quite chatty. He said that he had been educated by American Baptist missionaries. He also said that the administration of the area under the British was primarily by the Burmese with only a few British officials. The administration had continued to function after the British were defeated and the Japanese pretty much left it to continue functioning under their supervision.

4 THE CAPTORS

In writing this history of three years of my life I assure you all the events I describe are in sequence. What I can't vouch for is the amount of time that separated the events. My memory is a little fuzzy and I didn't have a watch or a calendar.

I think we left the shelter where I spent the night about nine o'clock in the morning. We walked on a mud road with an occasional house on either side and, after two hours, arrived at what was obviously the marketplace of the area. The market place was very busy and I saw many stalls displaying fruit and vegetables. I was taken into the poultry department and put into an empty chicken coop. The coop was about 3 feet wide and 8 feet tall. To get in I had to squeeze through a small door, which was then latched as if I was no more dangerous than a chicken. Of course, they were right. Absent a network of people loyal to the British, and willing to risk their lives helping me escape, my chance of reaching friendly territory was nil. A crowd gathered to look at me and I realized I was an oddity because they had never seen a white man who was not in a superior position.

Time passed and eventually I saw George Wilson being escorted in my direction. In a short time George was in the chicken coop next to me. I inquired about his health. He said he was fine and he asked about mine. With those civilities over we immediately started to work out a story that would keep us from contradicting each other if and when we were questioned separately.

We both felt that name, rank and serial number might not cut it. We decided that we would maintain that we had just arrived in the theater of operation, this was our first mission and the only person we knew on the plane was the pilot. To keep from divulging his name we decided to rename him Captain George Douglas and in all our planning thereafter we referred to him as George Douglas. We didn't know each other too well because we had just met on this mission. We agreed that we didn't know anything about the strength of the American Air Force in India because we had just arrived.

We were still aligning our stories when we were taken out of the chicken coops and marched about an hour through a small city. We ended up at a large two-story building. We were taken to the second floor where we were put into an enormous jail cell. We were the only occupants. It was here that George mentioned his main concern about our impending questioning. The United States had developed the Norden bombsight, a very advanced and accurate device. All bombardiers had taken an oath not to divulge, or even discuss, anything about this very secret weapon. I knew he was concerned about his oath so I reminded him that I had never seen the bombsight nor had he ever discussed it with me. We agreed that, if it was possible, I would answer all questions concerning the bombsight.

I tried to think of any other information that I had that would be of any value to the Japanese. I was unsuccessful. Possibly, by some stretch of the imagination, the number of B-17's in India could be important. After we were shot down, the 88th Reconnaissance Squadron had only the two planes that did not complete the mission. It was more than a little humbling to realize I knew so little.

I had joined the Air Force in February of 1941. I had learned celestial navigation and dead reckoning at the University of Miami. I believe I was made Cadet Captain because of my superior ability to give the drill commands: forward march, halt, right face, left face and about face. The only thing I learned other than celestial navigation is that rank dictates who gives the orders and who takes them.

I shared with George my assessment of myself and he confirmed that our knowledge and training was almost identical. We then wondered whether the Japanese junior officers were similarly uninformed or would the interrogators expect us to be a jackpot of valuable information. While it was demoralizing to realize my insignificance, it was somewhat comforting to know that there was no way I was going to adversely affect the war effort by anything I said.

In the morning I was visited by the old man with whom I had tried to communicate using the Sears Roebuck catalog. He spoke excellent English and explained that he was a pensioner of the British. He wanted me to promise that, when the British returned and saved me, I would inform them that he had been a good boy. I assured him I would be glad to vouch for him. He gave me his name, which I proceeded to forget because his concerns were ridiculous.

I had only a vague idea of where we were in relation to Rangoon. During the battle Doug was trying to reach cloud cover which was almost due north, yet as the Zeros attacked he had to fly the plane defensively. He was turning in the direction of attacking planes and lifting and lowering the wings of the plane to accommodate the men firing from the top and bottom turrets. The air battle lasted about 20 minutes and the speed of the B-17 is 280 mi./hr.,so I calculated we were 50 to 60 miles from Rangoon.

By walking through the city for about an hour we reached a very busy highway. I was told it was the road to "Pay-goo". (Pegu was the name of the city, located on the Irrawaddy River between Rangoon and Mandalay) This information was of no value because I had never seen a map of Burma that showed cities and topographical information.

To the navigator the whole world is flat like the ocean.

The "map" we use is a Mercator projection which is a blank piece of paper except for lines that represent latitude and longitude. Cities and targets are represented by a point created at the intersection of a line drawn through the latitude and one through the longitude.

We had been treated with respect by our jailers. I feel sure that through the grapevine everyone we encountered knew we were the airmen who had been captured. Our jailers had a somewhat brief conversation with someone who appeared to be a person of authority. While we stood there, George brought to my attention the fact that some of the trucks passing us were Fords and we also saw a couple of Jeeps. After the war, I learned that when the Japanese captured Rangoon they acquired millions of dollars of war supplies that were to be shipped to Chaing Kai-shek via the Burma road. The American officers in charge of the port facilities failed to destroy the supplies before retreating. After about an hour, the person of authority signaled a troop transport to stop.

George and I were put in the truck with six Japanese soldiers. The person of authority spoke to them and they made room for us. Our hands were not tied nor were we restrained in any way.

On the way to Rangoon the Japanese soldiers said what we thought was "do you speak Japanese ?", of course we responded inquiring whether they spoke English. The answer, if any was given, was negative.

George and I felt free to discuss our strategy for not giving any useful information during interrogation. The soldiers in the truck were the first Japanese that we had encountered. They were chatting and laughing amongst themselves as if they didn't have a worry in the world.

It took about two hours for us to reach Rangoon. We were escorted off the truck and into a bungalow. There were five officers seated around a table and they motioned us to sit on the floor. They talked amongst themselves and apparently asked us some questions in Japanese which we, of course, couldn't answer. They were eating and apparently had a discussion as to what would be appropriate food for Americans. One of them left the table and came back with a can of condensed milk. He opened it and gave it to George and me to share. I drank a little and passed it to George. I have no idea why we were taken to the bungalow.

George and I were then taken to the Rangoon City Jail and put into separate cells, too far apart for us to communicate.

June 5, 1942 New Orleans, Louisiana.

The day after I was shot down, my father reads in the Times Picayune that the United States had won a decisive victory at the Battle of Midway Island. The Navy under the command of Adm. Nimitz, has defended Midway Island. The Island would have become a launching point for the Japanese for an attack on Hawaii. He realizes that in the six months since Pearl Harbor the Navy has repaired its ships and the Pacific Fleet has destroyed the Japanese Navy.

He also notices an article about heavy bombers raiding Rangoon, which says the squadron was led by Capt. Frank D. Sharp and one plane was lost. He knows that the pilot of my plane was addressed as Doug Sharp. He feels that Frank D. and Doug Sharp are the same man and I was probably in his plane when he bombed Rangoon. He remembered discussing with my mother the raids on Myitkyina and decides to tell her about the raid on Rangoon. He wants her to know that as safe as the B-17 is, the plane is not invincible.

One plane was lost and he is thankful that it wasn't the one piloted by Capt. Doug Sharp.

Lonely Midway Repels Enemy, Dishes Out an Attack of Its Own

THIS IS THE TINY ISLAND OFF WHICH JAPS, I__   FIGHTING FRIDAY

—Photo by the Associated Press.

U.S. Bombers Blast Rangoon Docks by Daylight, Down Two Jap Fighters

(The Associated Press)

New Delhi, India, June 5.—The United States Army air force bombed shipping and docks at Rangoon in occupied Burma in daylight yesterday and suffered its first loss of a heavy bomber since it began operating from India.

Two and perhaps three Japanese fighting planes were shot down when 12 of them attacked, and heavy anti-aircraft fire was encountered, a communique said.

The exact type of plane lost was not specified but it was presumed to be a four-motored bomber such as used in previous Burma bombings.

(In Washington, a war department announcement of the attack said the bombers were led by Captain Frank D. Sharp and added that, because of a heavy overcast, it was impossible to determine the damage inflicted.)

The communique said:

"Heavy bombers with Captain Sharp leading, bombed Rangoon shipping and docks in daylight June 4. Overcast precluded observation of the resultant damage.

"Twelve fighters attacked. Two certainly and one probably were destroyed. Heavy attack was encountered. One of our own aircraft failed to return."

5 THE BEGINNING

The food I was given that night was as good as you would expect in most jails. It consisted of white rice, curry and a glass of tea. The bed was a slab of teak with a wooden pillow attached to it. The pillow was a half round with a 5 inch radius that extended the full width of the board. In the morning the Japanese guard serving the food bowed to me so I bowed to him. It occurred to me that this was some sort of a salute and I was quick to respond to any bow. There was a faucet with running water so I could sort of wash up. I knew that soon I would have to give a performance that would have a lot to do with the treatment I would receive during my incarceration. I decided to do exactly what I had been told was required under the Geneva Convention. I also realized that everything I said had to match the story on which George and I had agreed.

At midmorning I was ushered into a room where there was only one Japanese officer. He stood up and bowed and I immediately bowed. He waved me to the seat across from him. He was slightly older than me, but I couldn't tell his age. While his English was not perfect he certainly could make himself understood and could understand what I was saying. He said he was from Japanese Intelligence and that he wanted me to answer some questions. I immediately said that I was Kenneth F. Horner , I was a Second Lieutenant and my serial number was 0435393. He made me repeat the information slowly and carefully as he recorded it. He then instructed me to give him the name of the members of my crew. I knew this was the turning point. I had to establish some parameters for the interview, if I could.

In a raised voice I said, "I've already given you my name, rank and serial number and that is all I need to say under the Geneva Convention."

I paused momentarily.

" I can't answer your question anyway because I don't know the names of the crew of the plane I was in."

He looked at me for a few moments and I began to doubt my ability to lie convincingly. He then asked how I could not know the names of the crew. I told him the story George and I had concocted. I volunteered that the only person I knew on the plane was Capt. George Douglas. It was quite a long interview because he asked how I had arrived in India. That permitted me to talk about flying to all the different cities constituting the ferry route from Tampa, Florida to Karachi, India. I explained how, after resting for a day in Karachi, I was flown to Calcutta, India where I met the pilot Capt. George Douglas. What we talked about was really of no consequence. Eventually I was returned to my cell. A few moments later I saw George walk past my cell on the way to his interview. I hoped that he would fare as well as I thought I had.

To simplify the telling of my experiences in Rangoon Central Jail, I want to refer to the first intelligence agent as

"Number One." I can remember three others that spoke very little English and probably understood less. I won't waste time trying to describe them because they were inconsequential. Only their brief questioning interfered with the routine of the day. I only saw George when he walked past my cell. I assume we were in the last couple of cells because, other than the man who brought my food, I never saw any of the jail's staff. This was the first time I experienced solitary confinement. Even given satisfactory food and shelter, being alone for an extended period of time is very difficult. I spent my time carefully reviewing my interview with Number One, trying to convince myself that my story sounded plausible.

Two days after my first interview I was again taken into a room with Number One. As before, we saluted each other by bowing. I was surprised how insignificant his questions were, nevertheless I answered them as factually as I could so I wouldn't accidently contradict myself. Number One then dropped what he must have felt was a serious discrepancy in my testimony. He said Lt. Wilson had revealed that my name was really Jack instead of Kenneth. I told him Jack was my nickname.

He said, "Nickname? Nickname? What's nickname?"

I explained it was a name that people were generally called by close friends. I said as an example, "William is called Bill and Robert is called Bob."

Number One said, "Ah! so people named Kenneth are called Jack."

I said, "Not really. My name comes from a nursery rhyme."

Number One seemed to think a moment or two and then said, "Nursery rhyme?"

I said, "Yes. There is a nursery rhyme, which all children learn, about a little boy named Jack Horner and since my last name is Horner, friends started calling me Jack. The nursery rhyme is, 'Little Jack Horner, sat in a corner, eating a Christmas pie. He put in his thumb and pulled out a plum and said what a good boy am I !"

Number One said, "Say that again."

I repeated the nursery rhyme and he then asked, "Is that American nursery rhyme?"

I confessed that it was English. Our interviews never got much more serious than it did on this occasion, until a few days later.

As the time slowly past I began to think about 1,000 questions that I would like answered. Of course the most important one was "Will I survive and see my family again?" Other than when I was questioned the only sound I heard day in and day out was the guard calling my name to give me my meals. The Japanese, like the Chinese, have trouble with the letter "r" so my name was pronounced "HAWN-UH."

There were no restrictions on what I could do in my cell. To keep from becoming depressed I did calisthenics several times a day and tried to figure out how the Norden bombsight worked. Actually, what I was trying to determine and rehearse was what I would say if I were given a chance to explain the workings of the bombsight. I knew it had to be plausible, however , being convincing is difficult to do when you are describing something that you have never seen, touched or discussed.

I eventually came to the conclusion that the bombardiers, after training, really didn't know how the bombsight worked. What they knew is what data they must enter so that the bombsight could calculate the precise moment the bombs should be dropped. I knew that for some small amount of time the pilot surrendered the control of the aircraft to the bombardier. The bombardier then used the bombsight to stabilize the plane. I believe this was accomplished with a series of knobs that fixed the speed and drift of the plane. I felt they must also have to put in the weight of the bombs. He would then have a telescope with a crosshair that he would fix on the target. He would then press "on" and keep the crosshair on the target and the bombsight would calculate the precise moment to release the bombs.

I suspect most people who experience solitary confinement react in pretty much the same way. A feeling of helplessness and hopelessness is almost overwhelming. To keep from becoming depressed I began to fantasize about my happy return to my family. Reality overtook fantasy immediately. I could conjure up very pleasant scenarios about returning home though I realized it was only a dream.

I started to imagine what my parents must be experiencing. I had been captured on June 4 and it was now June 20th or 21st. I assume that my parents had received word from the government that I was a POW. I knew they would keep up a brave front. My younger brother, Harry, was on a Merchant Marine ship in the

South Pacific. My younger sister, Carmen, was married to a Naval Petty Officer. My father was a retired railroad engineer and an avid reader of world news. My mother was a devout Catholic and believed strongly in the power of prayer. It has been said that those who remain at home also suffer. I knew that would be true for my family.

I knew that their normal way of life would be suspended when they received the telegram advising them that I was missing in action or a prisoner of war. I also realized their life would be spent seeking information and comforting each other.

As a kid I had been told by my peers that when people are drowning they review their whole life. That may or may not be true because after the person drowns he is not available for questioning. I can attest to the fact that someone incarcerated as I was certainly reviews his life. At 14 years old I became a caddy at the City Park golf course in New Orleans.

The first half of the 1930s was the height of the Great Depression. In 1935 Pres. Roosevelt created several government programs to create jobs and income for the unemployed. One of the programs was the National Youth Administration which provided jobs for youths between 16 and 22 years old. My jobs included being a librarian at the New Orleans Central Library. I also had a job as a laboratory technician in the pathology department of the Marine Hospital. I went to Loyola University in New Orleans on a work scholarship and my jobs included serving as a librarian in the Medical and Pharmacy library and serving as secretary and receptionist for the Jesuit priest's residence. After due consideration, I decided that, although I received praise from my bosses, my job performances were only worth a C minus. I learned fast and did a good job, however I realize now that I was lazy. I quit school after my sophomore year. My grades were so-so, even though I exceled in mathematics and chemistry.

I was very fortunate at 19 to get a job working as a bench chemist for the Freeport Sulfur Company. The sulfur mines were located at the Grande Ecaille salt dome 65 miles south of New Orleans on the West side of the Mississippi River. I lived in a boarding house in Port Sulphur and went to work each morning via a motor launch which operated 24 hours, 7 days a week transporting employee's. My boarding house was owned by the company and housed single male accountants, chemists and physicists. Technical married employees were provided a house.

The town of Port Sulphur was owned by the company and did not provide a great deal of entertainment for its young single employees. There was a motion picture theater, a bowling alley and a well patronized barroom just outside of the city limits. The main entertainment available was playing penny ante poker and listening to the radio about the war in Europe. The British were losing the battle for France and the evacuation from Dunkirk was completed, exactly 2 years before I was captured, on June 4, 1940.

Ships that were loaded with sulfur had been torpedoed and sunk by German submarines in the Gulf of Mexico. I thought that in a short time we would declare war on Germany. I was told that my job analyzing sulfur would keep me from being drafted. I knew, however, if the United States declared war on Germany I would volunteer for some branch of the service. At the same time, with the help of a physicist, I perfected an easier and quicker method of determining the amount of carbonaceous matter in sulfur samples. After months of running duplicate samples, the licensed chemist decided to discontinue the old, time consuming method of testing and use the new method. The time to do the testing was reduced from 35 hours a week to eight hours a week.

I had originally been hired by a senior corporate officer in New Orleans. When he learned of the new testing method and my involvement, he suggested that I go back to school full-time and arrange to do the necessary work in Port Sulphur at night on Tuesdays and Thursdays. It was an opportunity of a lifetime and I was too lazy or too stupid to take it. I still cling to the excuse that I refused the offer because the work was too sedentary. In any case, I quit my job and joined the Army Air Corps as a Flying Cadet.

6 TALKING THE TALK

A day or so after my self-analysis, I was moved to a large cell. It was 20 feet wide and 50 feet long. There was a 2-foot raised platform on one side of the wall that contained a toilet and, adjacent to it, a faucet. I thought my cell was being upgraded until, after a few minutes, the guards brought in George Wilson. George and I were delighted to see each other and immediately started to compare our experiences with the interrogators. They were quite similar and we were convinced that our stories had been accepted. We discussed Number One. He certainly seemed to be a person of some rank yet his questioning had been innocuous.

George did relate that after he was questioned by one of the more inept questioners he was taken to a room where a man was being tortured. The man was suspended from the ceiling by a rope tied to his wrist. His arm had been turned so that it was behind his back. His feet could barely reach a table where he could relieve the pain in his arm and shoulder. George said it was obvious he was being questioned because the questioner pushed his feet off the table and he bounced around trying to regain his footing. George said he stood there with his Japanese questioner a minute or two and was then returned to his cell.

A few days later, fourteen Chinese men were put in our cell. Twelve of the men were quite old and did not speak English. The youngest man, whose name was Koo, appeared to be 35 or 40 years old and spoke good English. The other young man was named Chan and did not speak English at all. I don't know whether the Japanese had anything to do with it, but the Chinese moved as far from the door as they could and left the first 15 feet to me and George. Mr. Koo informed us that they had been big supporters of the Chinese forces under Chiang Kai-shek. The records, which showed the significant amount of money they had contributed, were found by the Japanese. According to Mr. Koo, the custodian of the records should have destroyed them but failed to do so. He believed they were to be punished in some way but he had no idea what the Japanese would do.

Our jailers continued to feed George and me three meals a day in separate containers and each of us had a spoon with which to eat it. The Chinese received their food in two large containers. This arrangement lasted about 30 days until the elderly Chinese were deported. At least that is what Mr. Koo understood from the Japanese guards. This left Mr. Chan, Mr. Koo, George and me as the occupants of this very large cell.

There was considerable discussion amongst us, including Mr. Koo translating for Mr. Chan, about the alleged deportation of the Chinese. Mr. Koo explained that it would take motor transport to reach the border of China and he doubted if the Japanese would go to that trouble and expense.

He felt that the guard had no knowledge of what happened and that the Chinese had probably been released into the city. I can't remember anyone offering a different opinion as to the fate of the Chinese.

AUTHOR'S NOTE:

Dateline July 7, 1942, New Orleans, Louisiana.

Over a month had passed since I'd parachuted into Burma.

My father has been to the store and, on returning, finds my mother sitting in stunned silence with a telegram in her hand. He tries to console her with the fact that "missing in action" means it is unknown whether or not I was taken prisoner or if I was hiding out with friendly natives. He realizes that a newspaper article the next day would alert all of their relatives and friends. He decides that for my mother's sake he would try to handle the calls without disturbing her. He also feels that he should call her sister, Julienne. He tells Julienne the news and she starts crying.

After a few moments he says, "Jeanne needs you. Please come as soon as you can."

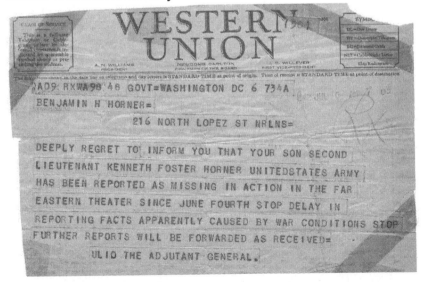

7 A NEW CELL MATE

After a few more days, a Japanese civilian was put into our cell. He said his name was Fujikee Tosiyome and he was or had been an Army photographer. Fujikee was quite friendly and told us the following story using a smattering of English and a great deal of sign language. According to him he had been a junior Army officer who had served his time and was released to become an Army photographer. One night he drank a great deal of Sake and became intoxicated. He was persuaded by a Burmese to create and sign a pass. According to Fujikee, the Burmese was caught and his pass discovered. He was subsequently arrested and put in our cell. Without a great deal of discussion amongst us we realized if Fujikee's story was right, he had committed the crime of aiding and abetting the enemy. That's a pretty serious charge and if he was found guilty would receive a very serious punishment. Of course all our minds switched back to the fate of the 12 elderly Chinese.

I think I had been a prisoner about ten weeks when an event occurred that clarified my position. The guards came and removed Mr. Chan from our cell.

A couple of hours later the guard returned and informed us that,"Mr. Chan cry, cry, cry, boom."

Fujikee talked to the guard and then said to us,"This is die man cell."

That kind of information tends to keep one awake at night, but eventually you realize there is nothing you can do to improve your lot except pray.

I remembered Henley's "Invictus" and recited to myself,"I thank whatever gods may be for my unconquerable soul." Each of the four of us handled the information in our own way.

As the days slowly past we adopted some sort of a routine for ourselves. The jailers were consistent. Each day the guard would shout "Hawn-uh" and give me my food. I exercised by doing calisthenics and there was still a great deal of conversation amongst us. We discussed family histories and the different cultures that existed in the countries that we had seen.

From Fujikee I learned the Japanese alphabet. As I recall the Japanese don't have vowels like A, E, I, O and U. They have, if I remember correctly, a 72 letter alphabet. They combine the consonants with the vowels so they have letters like ka, ke, ki, ko and ku. They repeat the combination with all the consonants and have a symbol for each letter. For instance the symbol for KU was very much like a big 7. If I had any linguistic ability at all I could have learned a lot of Japanese from Fujikee. Unfortunately, I never did well trying to learn a foreign language, I had taken courses which I barely passed in Spanish, French and German in high school. Not learning some Japanese was a tremendous missed opportunity.

At any rate, in this way, I passed my days and tried to remain hopeful.

8 THE INTERROGATION

I had been a prisoner for about two and a half months when George and I were called to the interrogation room. We were greeted by Number One who stood up and saluted. We saluted him back and he motioned us to sit down. I remember him rubbing his hand on his face to indicate he had noted our beards. He said that Lt. Wilson must tell him about the Norden bombsight. I recognized that this was the command performance for which I had prepared. I said,"Lieut. Wilson cannot discuss that with you because he took an oath not to divulge how it works. I did not take such an oath and I can tell you anything you want to know."

Number One looked at me for a few seconds and then said slowly,"All right, go ahead."

I said, "Some of what I have to say is so simple it may offend you."

Number One said, "Take your time. I like details."

I then explained that as the pilot approached a target he surrendered control of the plane to the bombardier who, with the use of the bombsight, stabilized the plane. I embarked on a very long explanation of the trajectory of a bomb when it is released from a speeding aircraft and the data that must be entered so the Norden bombsight can calculate the precise moment of release.

I continued to explain, "When a bomb is released from the plane it has a forward speed equal to the speed of the plane. How far it travels depends on its weight. If you threw two steel balls and one was lighter than the other because it had a hollow center, the lighter ball would go further. The weight of the bomb must be entered into the bombsight by means of a dial and a small keyboard. This of course can be done on the way to the target, long before the actual bomb run. When released a bomb travels a short distance forward and then drops vertically to the target."

Number One opened his fountain pen and passed it and an analysis pad towards me, "Explain."

Instead, I closed the pen, put it in my right fist and said it was the bomb. I then opened my fist and dropped the "bomb" into my left hand. I then turned my hand so that my fingers held the fountain pen. I then slowly moved my left hand at a slight downward angle, away from my right fist. After about 18 inches I turned my hand and dropped the pen to the desk.

Number One made a statement, "I see that the weight of the bomb determines how far it travels before it drops vertically and the altitude of the plane is not important."

I said, "That is correct but the ground speed of the plane must be accurate. The instruments available to the pilot and navigator indicate the airspeed which is how fast the plane is moving in the air mass. The air mass, in relation to the ground, could be moving North, South,

East, West or any of the 360° of the compass. For example, if the plane was headed North and the wind was from the North, the ground speed would be less than the air speed.

If, on the other hand, you were headed South the ground speed would be greater than the airspeed. If the plane was headed East or West the ground speed and the airspeed would remain the same. The variance between the ground speed and airspeed is called the "drift". The Norden bombsight has a built-in drift meter which enables the bombardier to set the true ground speed. His final act is to place a crosshair on the target and track it till the bombs are released. If the bombardier does his job right, a bomb dropped from 30,000 feet could hit a flowerpot on the ground."

Number One said, "You seem to think some bombardier's good, some bad. Is Lieut. Wilson good?"

I remembered our story, "I really don't know. The only time I was with him when he dropped a bomb was the day we were shot down and I don't know whether or not he hit anything. I was too busy looking for the Zeros."

Number One dismissed us, "That's enough for now. You may return to your cell."

George and I saluted him and he returned the salute.

As soon as the guard locked us in and left, George said to me that I had divulged almost everything he knew about the Norden bombsight. I told him that in my opinion neither he nor any other bombardier knew anything about the true workings of the bombsight. I suggested what they had been taught was how to operate it. I only told Number One the data that I knew would have to be given to a bombsight to make it work. I also said the Japanese engineers have built aircraft and warships and didn't need the chicken shit information I had given them to build a bombsight. I also said if he didn't know any more than what I had said he should forget the stupid oath. After we discussed our situation we decided that if he was questioned again he was free to repeat the information I had given. Personally I wondered why, as a bombardier, he was required to take the oath. The senior officers who had decided what his proper behavior should be under questioning must have known that he might be subjected to torture or death because of his refusal to cooperate. I have no doubt that because of this he experienced more hopelessness than I did during our incarceration.

After about an hour, the guard who had announced the demise of Mr. Chan came to the door and announced, "Hawn-uh talk good."

This provoked a discussion amongst George, me and Mr. Koo, even Fujikee tried to participate. We finally concluded that the guard really didn't have any knowledge other than from conversations that he may have over heard. Of course my main concern was for George's state of mind. I asked George how he would have felt if the announcement had been, "Hawn-uh talk no good."

George replied he would have felt very depressed. I then suggested that we should feel somewhat optimistic because of the positive announcement. The four of us agreed and we returned to our monotonous daily routine.

About a week later, late in the afternoon, the guard came to our door, opened it and called for me and George to come out. When we got into the hall we immediately saw six soldiers armed with rifles. We stepped forward between them and they escorted us out to a waiting truck. The truck had long seats on each side, the soldiers seated themselves and indicated to us that we must sit on our backside on the floor. George sat down facing the back of the truck. I knelt down until one of the soldiers rather gently pulled my shoulder back to indicate he wanted me to sit on my ass facing forward.

The truck moved forward and George asked me, "What do you think?"

I remember answering, "I don't know, George. Try not to think."

After what seemed a very short ride we stopped and I could see we were beside a tall windowless brick wall. Everything I knew about firing squads I had learned from the movies and this wall appeared to be a classic site. The truck moved forward into the dimly lighted area and we had entered Rangoon Prison.

Since I accepted and believed that I was going to be executed, I can speak with authority about what one thinks and feels just prior to being killed. The answer is nothing. I must have gone into shock because I don't remember getting out of the truck, having any contact with my jailers or how I got to my cell.

I was awakened by George calling my name. We discovered that a vacant cell was between us, which caused us to speak louder than we thought prudent. We decided to wait silently for the next event.

Dateline August 26, 1942 - New Orleans

Three months after I parachuted into Burma, my parents received a letter from General G. C. Marshall, the Chief of Staff of the War Department expressing sympathy. He also said that it is possible that if I am a prisoner of war it will be reported through the International Red Cross. My father notes that there is only a possibility that the War Department will be notified.

The next day, August 26th , my father sees the picture

HEROIC FLYERS DECORATED

—ASSOCIATED PRESS WIREPHOTO

WASHINGTON, August 26.—This photo taken at an undisclosed location and released here today, shows Brig. Gen. Earl L. Naiden (right), acting commander of the United States Army Air Force in India, China and Burma, decorating Maj. Frank D. Sharpe (left) of Salem, Ore., and Lieut. Herbert F. Wunderlich of Williston Park, L. I., for heroism in fighting the Japanese over Burma. Wounded, they escaped from enemy-held Burma after the crash landing of their Flying Fortress.

of Capt. Douglas Sharp and Lieut. Wunderlich receiving the Silver Star. The article is a description of the June 4th battle and how Sharp and the co-pilot were eventually rescued.

He also learns that six of the crew bailed out of the B-17. The article reinforces his original statement to my mother that I was probably a prisoner of war or hiding with friendly Burmese.

He feels it's in his and my mother's best interest to continue believing that I am alive.

9   THE PRISON

My cell was quite large. It was 15 feet by 20 feet with a 3-foot by 7-foot steel prison door in a 15-foot wall. The floor was concrete and the only thing in the room was a 5 gallon gasoline can from which the top had been removed. The can was to serve as my toilet. My door opened to a 4-foot balcony that ran the length of the building. I was in the second cell and to reach it the guards had to come up a stairway and walk 20 feet to my cell door. From my cell door I could see over the wall and into the adjacent compound. The cell was unique because there was nothing except the prison door between me and the outside world.

I heard someone coming up a stairway and, in a moment, three men appeared before my door. There was a very large Burmese, a small Chinese and a Japanese guard. The guard opened the door and motioned me out. He then motioned to the Burmese to hit me. He struck me on the left side of my head with his open hand and then, with his left hand, he struck the right side of my head. The guard was screaming and motioned him to keep going so he repeated, and repeated, and repeated. The guard was acting sort of hysterical.

He took off his belt and struck me with the buckle end. He repeated this several times on my arms and shoulders and then he aimed at my head. On his second swipe at my head the strap went around my head and when he jerked it I was pulled slightly forward. I bowed. I saluted. He pushed me back into my cell and motioned to the Chinese to feed me. I was given a cake plate with some rice, a spoon and some soup. He also gave me a tin can full of water. As the entourage moved towards George's cell, I put my food down and returned to the prison door.

I could hear George being given the same punishment I had received so I shouted for him to bow. I am not sure that George heard me, however the guard certainly did. After George was given his food and put back in his cell, the entourage returned to my door. I immediately saluted but that did no good. The door was opened, I was motioned to come out and the Burmese delivered his very best blow to my head. This was the first time during my captivity that I was physically abused by the Japanese and it certainly wasn't life-threatening. This was also my first encounter with the guard named Weno. I committed to memory the Japanese characters on his hat for possible future use. After a few minutes I called George to ask if he was all right.

He answered, "Not too good. I think a part of the

buckle pierced my eardrum. It hurts like hell and I can't hear out of my right ear."

I said, "If we get out of here alive, George, I'll make that son of a bitch pay for what he did!"

Sometime during the morning I realized that my plate was to be used over and over and should be cleaned in preparation for the next meal. I decided to wipe it dry with one of my socks and thereafter keep it face down over the spoon until my next meal. This would also give my sock a chance to dry. I decided I would sleep with my clothes on and use my shoes as a pillow.

I don't remember anything about my first night in Rangoon prison. My second night was quite a revelation. My wardrobe consisted of jockey shorts underwear, a pair of pants, a shirt, two socks and a handkerchief. My clothes were also my only worldly possessions other than my dining equipment. After an uneventful evening meal, the temperature dropped 20 or 25 degrees and hundreds of mosquitoes arrived to feast on me. The Scottish poet, Robert Burns wrote that the best laid plans of mice and men often go astray and he was right.

While I had planned to sleep in my clothes, I discovered what I needed was to insulate myself from the cold concrete. I took off my pants and folded them as if they were going to be draped over a hanger. I then laid them on the floor to create a palette that was 7 inches wide and about 30 inches long. The palate provided four thicknesses of cloth between the floor and my upper body. I used the shirt to cover my head and shoulders to keep off the mosquitoes. It is remarkable how the human body can adapt and adjust to adverse conditions. I slept fitfully and without moving through the long night. When daylight came the mosquitoes left. I put on my clothes and did some deep breathing exercises, and was as prepared as one could be, under these conditions, for the day.

A couple of hours after dawn my food was delivered. The guard, who was not Weno, stepped in front of my cell and turned facing me. I saluted, that is, bowed, and he saluted me back. I retrieved my cake plate and tin can from the floor and the Chinese gave me my food and water. I remained standing with my plate and cup until they moved on to George's cell. There was no discernible difference in this routine for the next three or four days.

I had begun doing calisthenics very early after being captured and I know they were helping me physically, but I had to do something mentally to pass the time.

In grammar school I skipped the grade where children are taught multiplication. The promotion certainly had an adverse effect on my ability to do arithmetic. I felt that if I forced myself to concentrate on an arithmetic problem time would pass faster. I started with two digits multiplied by one digit. An example would be 69 multiplied by 8. I did many of these and, while I could not in any way check the accuracy of my answers, I began to feel very confident they were correct. I next advanced to two digits multiplied by two digits. An example would be 65 multiplied by 36. I spent a great deal of time doing these exercises and they certainly had a salutary effect. I eventually graduated to three digits multiplied by two digits and, eventually, three digits multiplied by three digits. The only real shortcoming was I never knew if I succeeded in getting the right answer. Nevertheless the concentration was intense. I remember one time when George called me I felt momentarily that he was interfering in my work.

On about the fifth day, a Japanese officer, accompanied by a guard, came to my cell door. I saluted and after they saluted, I was given a tablet and a pencil. At the top of the tablet was the question, "Why US want war?"

They moved on to George Wilson's cell and I began to wonder what the hell I was going to write. I knew I was going to write something even though, in a situation like mine, movie heroes defy the enemy, are tortured, do jujitsu and then escape.

When we felt that the coast was clear George and I discussed how we should explain why the US wanted to go to war. We joked about how the government had failed to get our permission to get involved in this conflict. I don't think history is taught in high school anymore, but at Warren Easton Boys High School we were required to take classes in history. I remembered that the Monroe Doctrine, which was written just after we defeated England in the war of 1812, warned the powerful European countries to cease colonizing efforts in the Western Hemisphere. I wrote that the United States felt that Japan was threatening some of our possessions. I did not attach any importance to anything I said and apparently that was a satisfactory answer because I never heard anything about what I had written.

What was important was that I could tear out pages

of the tablet and do several math problems mentally and then check them with a pencil and paper. As long as a multiplier was one digit I was perfect. When the multiplier was two digits I had a couple right and a couple wrong. When I graduated to three digits multiplied by three digits I made the mental calculations and recorded the number. When I solved the problem with the pencil and paper, I wasn't surprised to find out that there was no resemblance between the two answers. I now knew that I wasn't very good at solving the problems, nevertheless I had whiled away several hours without a depressing thought.

I mentioned before that through my door I could see into the next compound. One day I saw several Japanese and about 10 or 12 inmates standing around some sort of seat. The men were wearing loincloths. I saw one of the men remove his loincloth and sit on the seat for about a minute. This act was repeated by all of the men. There is no doubt in my mind that there were mosquitoes captured in the seat below them and the Japanese were trying to infect them a fever. When George and I discussed it we agreed that Japanese doctors were trying to make the men sick with some sort of fever so they could treat it.

The days were long and the nights painful so I was delighted when the guards took George and me from our cells. We were taken to the front guard room of the prison and turned over to a contingent of four armed soldiers. They marched us about a mile and we entered a large cleared area. As we entered we walked past a company of Burmese soldiers and were made to stand facing a podium. I noticed on the left side of the podium there were two British soldiers and besides them a couple of Chinese soldiers. In the line that we were in, facing the podium, there were two Indian soldiers and a whole hodgepodge of Burmese officials.

After about 10 minutes the soldiers were marched into the area between the two lines. They did a left face and were facing the podium. There were speeches made by the Japanese and the Burmese, which I must confess I did not understand. While we were standing there George and I were presented with a piece of paper that they required us to sign. Without further ado we were returned to our cells.

Of course George and I had absolutely no idea what had just occurred. We agreed that we had witnessed a ceremony wherein Japan recognized Burma as an independent state. We also felt we should be very proud of ourselves because at our young age we had served as United States Ambassadors to Japan and had witnessed and certified Burma's independence.

We later learned that Japan had created an entity called The Greater East Asia Co-Prosperity Sphere and we had participated in the ceremony wherein Burma joined the Sphere.

10 A NEW LIFE

After two weeks of absolute misery, we were moved to Block #5. You can't imagine the thrill of finding that my new cell had a wood floor. After the guards left I found that there was an empty cell between me and George. We soon learned that the schedule of the day was pretty much the same as we had been experiencing. The food, however, was slightly different and practically indigestible. I later learned that the British referred to the soup as "jyp-oh" which I understand is a Hindustani word for stew. A meal consisted of rice and jyp-oh. The jyp-oh we had been getting was a very thin vegetable soup. The jyp-oh we now received had something that looked like corn in it. This corn looked exactly the same both before and after it was digested.

Each morning, my door was opened so I could race downstairs to a trough and empty the 5-gallon can that served as my toilet. The guards would continuously shout for me to hurry. To make the best of the situation, I welcomed it as good exercise. The first night we learned from fellow prisoners that we were not permitted to sit or lie down during the day. Apparently the guards patrolled in front of the cells and would slap the hell out of anyone caught breaking the rule. Since I had the luxury of sleeping on the beautiful wood floor I had no trouble standing up throughout the day. In addition, by tapping on the wall the inmates would alert everyone when the guard was patrolling. After about two weeks we were transferred to Block #3.

I remember saying at the beginning of this memoir, when I was in Calcutta, that being in the Air Force was the best way to fight a war. I now realize that being an airman was, if you were to become a prisoner of war, the best way.

There is a saying that every shoe doesn't fit every foot and certainly my experiences were unique. What is fairly common is that after a mission to bomb a target or to give ground support to troops, a damaged plane generally flies a good distance before crash landing. As a result, the airmen are captured by civilians or troops who have not been on the receiving end of his attack. In my case, we had traveled almost 100 miles from the time we dropped the bombs to where I bailed out of the plane. Except for a few bumps along the way my path to prison had been rather easy. I entered Block #3 in excellent health.

The other prisoners of war I met in Block #3 had not been so lucky. They were taken prisoner after battles that had large casualties on both sides.

Although I was in the China Burma India Theatre of Operations, I really knew very little about it. I had more knowledge of the European Theater of Operation. So that you might better understand how my fellow prisoners reached Block #3, I have written a brief history of Japanese, British and Chinese troops.

In early December, 1941 the Japanese were at war

with China. Japanese battleships had formed a successful blockade of the Chinese coast and their troops were driving the Army, under Chiag Kai-shek, to the West. The Chinese received their supplies, equipment and armaments via the 700 mile Burma Road which ran from the city of Rangoon to Kunming, China. In the 1930s King Rama IX of Siam (now Thailand) became an ally of Emperor Hirohito and the Japanese, by agreement, assembled a sizable Army in Siam. From their bases they could launch an attack to take Malaya and Singapore (300 miles to the south). They could also start a campaign to occupy Burma. The British had been at war with the Germans for over two years, but during that time they had created a major army in Burma, which they believed would stop the Japanese if they ever tried to reach India. Britain also reinforced Singapore, which was called the "Gibraltar of the East." The city was considered invincible because major armaments had been installed facing the ocean.

Attacks from the North were considered impossible because of the dense and impenetrable jungle. There were no tanks or portable cannons, but there were probably 40,000 trained soldiers with small arms.

On December 7, 1941 Japan launched their aerial attack on Pearl Harbor. Almost simultaneously they launched an attack on Malaya. On December 8, 1941 both the United States and Great Britain declared war on Japan. On February 1, 1942 Singapore capitulated to the Japanese. At the same time, the British were retreating from the Japanese and they crossed the Sittang River at a bridge located a short distance north of Moulmein. During the delaying action many soldiers were killed or wounded. Eventually the bridge was blown up leaving wounded and exhausted soldiers on the East side of the river.

On February 24, 1942 these people were captured and moved to Moulmein prison. During the four months that elapsed before they were moved to Rangoon prison, the officers were separated from the enlisted men and were treated humanely. The British Other Rank (BOR) were treated horribly. They were incarcerated in an overcrowded cell with 5 gallon cans to serve as toilets. They lived in absolute filth. The stink of human waste was unbearable. Food and water was very limited and the only relief from the flies was darkness. They were in bad shape when they reached Rangoon Central Prison. As prisoners died in Rangoon I frequently heard the remark "He was one of the Moulmein crowd."

The retreating forces bypassed Rangoon and crossed the Irrawaddy River at Pegu. Roadblocks were set up as the British retreated north on the Pegu-Mandalay Road and I'm sure that the Japanese took prisoners from these engagements, although I don't remember meeting any. Most of the prisoners in Block #3 came from a battle in the oil fields at Yenangyaung. Sergeant Major Tim Finnerty and his men had fought 11 hours waiting for Chinese troops under the command of Gen. "Vinegar Joe" Stillwell to reinforce them. Help never came and he and his men were among the Allied forces (Chinese, British, Indian and Gurkha) captured on Sunday, April 15, 1942.

It was almost 3 weeks before these prisoners reached Rangoon jail on May 5, 1942. For the first four or five days

Sergeant Major Finnerty and his men had been confined in a bungalow without food, water or medical attention. During that time some wounded died and were passed out the door to the Japanese. It became difficult to breathe as human waste accumulated on the floor. They were then tied together and forced to walk to the Irrawaddy River. This was a death march and as men dropped out they were shot. They were in bad shape when they reached Rangoon prison.

Rangoon prison had been built by the British in 1908 to house criminals. It consisted of eight large buildings located around a pump house like spokes of a wheel. The buildings were separated from each other by a 15-foot road with a 9-foot fence on each side. The road between Block #1 and Block #8 led to the front of the prison where a building housed the Japanese guards. Each block had a large water trough, a small area with a tin roof designated as a kitchen, and a large covered area designated as the latrine on one side of the building. On the other side was a large area which was used for growing vegetables.

The Allied prisoners were separated by race. The Chinese were in Block #1, the Gurkhas were in Block #2, British and American in Block #3, Block #4 was empty when destroyed by a bomb. Block #5 was for new prisoners and solitary confinement. In 1943, Block #6 began receiving survivors of the Wingate Raiders (Chindits) and British and American airmen. Indians were in Block #7. Block #8 was empty until February, 1945 when Allied airmen from Block #5, including the B-29 crewmen, were released from solitary confinement.

11 BLOCK #3

When I awoke my first morning in Block #3 I felt I knew myself, physically and mentally, and was prepared to cope with anything that would be required of me. The first business of the day was roll call (Tenko). The British lined up with the tallest man at the far right and the shortest man at the far left. They felt that George should stand next to the shortest man and that I would stand next to him. The guard indicated that we should be arranged by height regardless of nationality. When we understood what he wanted the formation was rearranged so that George was at the far right and I was trying to find my proper position in the line. When I tried to position myself about the center of the formation the officers kept saying, "further down."

I ended up at the very end of the line because I was the shortest of all the officers. This was a revelation to me because I always thought I was average height. I think the guard must have recognized my dilemma because he waited patiently until I found my place and then we proceeded with the roll call.

Finding out that I was short was the beginning of a learning curve that lasted three years. After our morning meal, Brig. Hobson briefly explained to George and me what he and the Japanese would expect from us. He would treat us, essentially, as if we were Second Lieutenants in the British army and we would respect him as if he were a Brigadier General in the United States Army. He explained that the Japanese required the officers to participate in work parties and we would be assigned to one the next day.

The two-story building in Block # 3 was approximately 35 feet wide and 200 feet long. 6" x 6" bars of teak wood separated a 6-foot alley from the rest of the building. The largest section was then divided by teak wood bars into three rooms which measured roughly 24' x 60'. These rooms were not locked. What was locked was the steel door at the end of the alley. During the night we had access to 30 gallon drums located in the alley where we could relieve ourselves. I mentioned these boring details because the contents of the 30 gallon drums were fertilizer that the garden party had to distribute.

The other job for the work party was to break new ground for additional vegetable beds. The garden was quite large and had been planted so that while we planted a new crop we would harvest eggplants from the old bushes. These were used to make our daily ration of "Jyp-oh". I never encountered any meat although I was told that some was added. To me, the "Jyp-oh" was eggplant soup. The officers work party consisted of 10 to 12 young men under the age of 23. We shared the work, good jobs and nasty jobs, and developed a feeling of camaraderie.

As unpleasant as some of the tasks were, they were far better than solitary confinement and idleness.   We worked four hours in the morning with a 10 minute break every hour. After an hour for lunch we worked an additional three hours.

In the garden area there was a cluster of trees around an open well.   On the breaks we went to the trees for shade, conversation and a chance to clean up. It was here that I met Kuma, a young Japanese soldier. He wore a wristwatch and his main job was to advise us when our rest period (Yatsuma) started and ended. We were required to add "San" to his name so that "Kumasan" translates to Mr. Kuma. I never saw him strike anyone and he certainly was a very lenient task master.

One day I was talking to Lt. Robin Steward, a Scotsman who had celebrated his 20th birthday in prison, when I noticed a heavy irregular piece of steel on the ground.

I pointed to it and said, "I bet I can throw that chunk of steel further than you can."

Robin said, "You're on."

I drew a 6-foot circle and invited him to stand in the circle and toss the steel. Robin picked up the steel, stepped into the circle and threw the steel a very short distance. I remembered how the shot put is supposed to be thrown.

I stood at the very far edge of the circle and put my right hand with the steel on my shoulder. I extended my left arm as I had seen done, raised my left leg, hopped forward on my right leg to gain some momentum, rotated my body and pushed the steel with my right arm. I set a mark at least four times farther than the one set by Robin.

When I declared myself the winner, Robin said, "No you aren't. Two out of three!"

Robin copied my technique and eventually won at best three out of five and everyone in the work party participated in the shot put. It occurred to me that the situation, no matter how grim, can be improved. I noticed that Kuma wanted to join in the activity but didn't because he was afraid he might be seen by other guards.

This particular part of the prison became a popular gathering place on Yatsuma days.

12 MY CREW

In early September some new prisoners arrived. I was delighted to find out they were the four enlisted personnel from my B-17. The men were Master Sergeant Al Maloc, Sgt. Eli Gonsalves, Sgt. Harold Cummings and Pvt. Smith Radcliff. They were in excellent condition. They had been confined with a Chinese General named Chi. Because of General Chi's kindness and the Japanese's tolerance they had provisions of coffee, cream, sugar, some bread and cheese, and some cookies. They also had pots and eating utensils. They invited George and me to join them for coffee after the evening roll call. I knew their way of life was going to change dramatically. We joined them for coffee and conversation.

We learned that after we jumped Sgt. Maloc succeeded in putting out the fire and the plane, even without our weight in the front, continued to slowly lose altitude.

After a period of time they were ordered to bail out. They landed somewhere near Mandalay. Sgt. Cummings also reported that the Zero I shot at went down. It was a great evening and we ended up singing "You Are My Sunshine."

I don't know if most men remember when they became a "man". I know the precise moment, because it occurred the day after having coffee with the enlisted personnel.

Sgt. Cummings approached me and said "May the Sgt. speak to the Lieutenant?"

I responded, "Certainly, Sgt. Cummings."

He said, "Sgt. Maloc has reprimanded me for calling you by your first name. Please advise me how you wish me to address you."

I said, "There are only six of us Americans here so I don't think we need to worry about rank, Harold. When you see Sgt. Maloc ask him to come see me."

When Sgt. Maloc approached me I said, "You know Sgt. Maloc that Sgt. Cummings felt that you reprimanded him unnecessarily. We are only six Americans and I don't think we need to maintain rank under these circumstances."

Sgt. Maloc responded with quite a speech, "Lieutenant Horner, we have been flying together for a while now. You and Lieutenant Wilson have certain luggage and equipment that has to be carried and stored in the plane. You don't have to do that because I do it for you. I also make certain that a parachute for each of you is in the proper place. I am responsible for the condition of the plane. If it is a long flight I arrange for food and drink.

I've often wondered why I am in a subservient position and you are so privileged. I believe it is because, at times, we enlisted men encounter situations that we're not equipped to handle. We are in that situation now and I am relying on you, your training, education and rank to get me out of this mess alive. I don't want to be your equal Lieutenant Horner because I'm depending on you to do your job."

I replied, "For your sake and mine I hope I can live up to your expectations. Advise your men that I am the commanding officer and must be treated as such. If you have a problem with the British, advise me and I will address it. Your welfare and health are my primary concern. If you need me, call me."

Sgt. Maloc defined the role I was supposed to play and I knew he was exactly right. I never again lost sight of my responsibility.

I found George Wilson and asked him which of us should be the commanding officer. Since his health had begun to deteriorate he agreed that I was the Senior Lieutenant. As new American enlisted personnel arrived they all addressed me as Lieutenant. The British Other Rank addressed me as Mr. Horner.

I tried my best to be friendly with everyone, however I didn't fraternize with subordinates. As time went by Sgt. Maloc and I became very close friends. He gave me a very fine pocketknife that he had acquired in Mandalay.

LOUISIANA FLIER IS DECORATED FOR 'HIGH GALLANTRY'

(The Associated Press)

Washington, Oct. 25. — Four army fliers whose bomber carried out a solo attack in Burma and shot down at least four Japanese fighters before being disabled have been awarded the silver star decoration, the department announced today, for "gallantry of the highest order."

A report of the action by Brigadier General Earl L. Naiden, American air commander in India, said the four were:

Staff Sergeant Albert L. Malok, engineer and gunner, Hellertown, Pa.

Sergeant Harold E. Cummings, radio operator and gunner, Monroe, La.

Sergeant Elias E. Gonsalves, gunner, 1132 Bellview, Los Angeles,

which last June 4 blasted freighter despite the opposition four enemy Zero fighters. Head back to its base in India, t bomber at one time fought swarm of 23 Japanese fight planes, and bagged four or mo

One of the crew, Private Fir Class Francis J. Teehan, Foo ville, Wis., was killed while ma ning a machine-gun turret. Mal and Cummings were wounded.

Then Major Frank D. Sha Salem, Ore., the commander, a

Dateline October 25 1942, New Orleans, Louisiana.

Four months after the air battle, my father sees the following headline in the paper: "Louisiana man receives Silver Star." The article refers to Sgt. Cummings. It also mentions Sergeants Maloc and Gonsalvez and Private Smith Radcliff.

These are the four men who jumped out of Captain Sharp's plane, after the fire was extinguished, and shortly before he crash landed. It also states that Private Tehan was awarded the medal posthumously.

He could now account for seven members of the crew. Two had reached friendly territory, one had been killed and four were reported as prisoners of war. He tried to conceive of a reason why, if we were prisoners, George and I weren't reported as such. It was increasingly difficult to pretend he thought I was alive.

He decided to comfort my mother as best he could.

She continued to pray.

13 TARGET RANGOON

In Block # 3 Brig. Hobson was the senior officer and as such he or his adjutant dealt with the Japanese. His adjutant was Major Nigel Loring, who was serving in the British Frontier Force when he was taken prisoner. He was very astute in dealing with the Japanese and administering the compound.

They were well aware that one of our work parties had built slit trenches at the front gate to protect the guards in the event the jail was bombed, but no provisions had been made for the prisoners. Their request for permission to build slit trenches for the prisoners was denied. There had not been any Allied aircraft over Rangoon since our B-17 raid on June 4.

On December 21, 1942 I was assigned to take a work

party to do coolie labor at the docks. In accordance with standard procedure we stopped short of the gate to await clearance to leave. At that same time the air raid alarms sounded, I looked up and saw 7 B-25's.

I think the whole work party was looking up when I said, "Kumasan, if they drop those bombs now they'll just about hit us."

When we saw the flash of the bombs being released, Kuma shouted, "Hawn-uh" and signaled me to put the men in a slit trench.

They all got in, I got in, Kuma got in. The last thing I saw was the Japanese guard pointing and laughing at us for being frightened. Then the bomb struck the area where they had been standing. Kuma saw that two or three of the guards had been killed and he signaled me to get back to the compound as fast as I could. The men got out of the trench and we all ran back to Block #3. I told the work party to get lost in the compound. I must say I was very concerned, but there were no immediate repercussions.

On the next day, after Tenko, the front line was made to about-face and trade slaps to the face with the back line. The guards patrolled the lines to be certain that we were slapping each other hard enough. After about 20 minutes the guards disappeared and we stopped slapping each other.

Several good things resulted from this bombing. First, the Japanese quartermaster, who was a particularly nasty piece of business, was killed. The second thing was that the Japanese administration permitted us to dig slit trenches. The third thing was that the Japanese decided to leave the door open at the end of the passageway. This allowed us to relieve ourselves in the latrine area and consequently we did not collect urine to fertilize the garden.

When Sgt. Maloc and the three crew members arrived they had been assigned to a room where the Inniskillin Fusiliers were quartered. As a senior noncommissioned officer Sgt. Maloc was put in charge of the room. The same men were kept together when the slit trenches were assigned. I was assigned as the officer in charge of the trench. The rule was that when the air raid warnings sounded both of us would go to the trench. We would count the men entering the trench and would be the last ones in.

The air raid of December 21 was the beginning of an irregular pattern of day and night raids by B-24 and B-25 planes. The prison was struck several times. Once the outside perimeter wall was struck and we had to rebuild it. The same is true of two interior walls that I recall. One bomb destroyed the building in Block #4 which was unoccupied at the time. During a daylight raid two men who decided not to use slit trenches were killed in Block #3.

The routine in Block #3 did not change. There was no medicine for the sick and dying and insufficient food for the rest. Lack of vitamin B in the rice caused Beri Beri and lack of sanitation caused Dysentery. These, along with jungle sores, scabies and malaria caused misery and death. Despite the fact that our physical health was deteriorating, the routine remained the same. I was sent out as a member, or in charge of, work parties that grew vegetables, salvaged bricks from demolished buildings, created super bomb shelters and dug revetments at the airfield. For some reason, which I can't explain, I was never again sent to handle cargo at the docks.

There was a general feeling amongst the prisoners that the Japanese would not recognize Christmas as a holiday or Yatsuma day. They were right and work parties were sent out on December 25, 1942. Instead of good food, Christmas trees, family and gifts, I reminisced about the almost unbelievable visit I had with my father, mother and sister on Christmas Eve of 1941.

When the Japanese attacked Pearl Harbor I was at Hamilton Field in San Francisco. My B-17 was part of the 10th Air Force, 7th Bomb Group that was being sent to reinforce General McArthur in the Philippines. The first stop on the route was Hickam Airfield on the island of O'ahu. The 22nd Bomb Squadron left San Francisco on the evening of December 6 and was landing, or had landed, when the Japanese planes attacked Pearl Harbor. My Squadron, the 88th Recon, had been scheduled to land at Hickam Airfield the morning of December 8th. Instead, we were loaded with bombs and searched the Pacific Ocean looking for Japanese submarines. We returned to Muroc Lake Airfield, from where we continued patrolling the Pacific shoreline.

On December 24th we were ordered to MacDill Airfield in Tampa via Randolph Field in San Antonio, Texas. At about six o'clock we took off from Randolph Field and we encountered a tropical storm between New

Orleans and Tampa. The pilot decided to land in New Orleans. When I learned that he intended to spend the night, I asked for permission to leave the crew. He ordered me to report back to duty at 8:00 AM Christmas Day. I called my parents and my father came and took me home for Christmas Eve.

It was, without doubt, the best Christmas present that I ever received.

14 THE WORK PARTIES

Generally speaking, if we did our work, the regular soldiers that supervised us were friendly. One day I was in charge of a work party that was assigned to work on a revetment. A revetment is a hole in the ground to keep planes from being struck by shrapnel if a bomb lands near them. My job was not to work, but to see to it that the men worked. One of the Jap soldiers and I noticed one of my party who was obviously loafing.

We both ran to the spot above where he was digging and I started berating him, "What the hell is the matter with you, Hawkins. We don't want to help these bastards but we don't want to be caught fucking off. Stand at fucking attention and look sad. Pick up that spade and start digging." I then faced the soldier and bowed. He bowed back and we moved away from each other.

Sometime later, near lunchtime, it began to rain. The Japanese soldiers and my crew all took shelter in a building made of galvanized steel roofing. It was obviously meant to be a temporary structure because it had a dirt floor, some benches and a table with two chairs. We made ourselves as comfortable as possible. Some of the soldiers engaged my crew in conversation. One of them came to where I was sitting and, after I jumped up to attention, took me to the table and chairs He sat me in one chair and he sat in the other. He put his elbow on the table with his hand pointed to the sky and I knew he wanted to arm wrestle. By now, we were the center of attention. I put my elbow down and grasped his hand and we both slowly began to exert pressure. At some point I felt he was doing everything he could to win so I slowly let him push the back of my hand to the table. He jumped up and while I didn't know what he was shouting, I knew that he realized I had let him win. He sat down with the intention of wrestling again.

One of my crew asked, "What are you going to do now, Lt. Horner?"

I didn't answer because I was trying to think of a way to just barely win. When I felt he was doing his very best I equaled the pressure but did not put him down for a couple of seconds and then I slowly pushed him down. He immediately adjusted his chair and presented his left arm. I tried again to barely defeat him. As we wrestled the Japanese soldiers were loudly and happily giving him advice. When he got out of his chair another soldier took his place. Eventually I wrestled and defeated five different soldiers. They then motioned to me to get out of the chair and they continued wrestling each other. The first soldier that had wrestled looked around the building and asked "Meshi Ki(food)?"

I indicated we had no wood to cook our rice. He sent one of his soldiers and two of my crew away and they returned with food that was distributed to all my crew. The whole episode reminds me very much of the shot put contest between Robin Stewart and me. I realized that the Japanese were young men, away from home, bored and seeking entertainment.

Despite the work we were assigned, most prisoners had a great deal of extra time on their hands. Since I had a good pocketknife I decided to make a chess set. I didn't know how long it would take, still I worked diligently to complete it. While I was carving the set a young officer named Dennis Cooper showed a great deal of interest and said he would create a checkerboard so that we could play. I felt I did a very credible job of whittling. The pieces looked very good and Dennis and I played our first game. Dennis won. Not easily but he did win.

A couple of days later we had a chance to play a second game. The game lasted over two hours and, in the end, Dennis won. Several other people played chess so the board was kept pretty busy.

A couple of weeks later, Dennis defeated me for the third time.

I remember saying, "Dennis that was a lot of fun for you but it's not so much fun for me. I'm going to give you the chess set. All I ask is that you create a tournament, excluding me, and prove you're the best chess player in Block #3. I can then claim I am the second-best player."

I then began carving smoking pipes for George and me.

Dateline April 25, 1943, New Orleans, Louisiana.

George Wilson's father sends my father an article from the Fargo Forum that says Lieutenant George Wilson has been reported as a prisoner of war.

My father was very discouraged.

Since George and I parachuted at the same time, it was highly probable that our fate would be the same. He reasoned that, since I wasn't reported as a POW, I could still be alive and in friendly hands. He knew he was grasping at straws but only by keeping a modicum of hope could he continue to nurture my mother's faith.

Carmen had a baby and named him Edward Kenneth. Since the household was very busy with a new baby he decided to share with my mother the information about George Wilson.

They had ceased discussing me daily and she accepted the latest news calmly.

Only the long time she spent on her knees praying remained constant.

Long Silence On Fargoan Ended

Lieut. George H. Wilson, Missing In Burma Almost A Year, Now Jap Prisoner

On a day in June in 1942, a parachute dropped from a riddled Boeing bomber.

On the business end of that parachute was Lieut. George H. Wilson of Fargo.

Until yesterday, when The Fargo Forum received a special dispatch from the United Press, there had been no word of him.

But yesterday, a Domei (Japanese news agency) broadcast recorded by the United Press listening post in New York brought out the name of Lieut. George H. Wilson, 28, "Boeing bomber pilot," as among the prisoners held by the Japanese in Burma.

Lieutenant Wilson, son of Mr. and Mrs. Charles V. Wilson, 1203 Seventh st S, participated in one of the striking operations that have been added to the great sagas of the war in the Southwest Pacific.

* * *

LIEUT. GEORGE H. WILSON

15 THE B-25's

Allied planes were being shot down by the Japanese and new prisoners were sent to solitary in Block #5. After a couple of months, they were released into Block #3 and after August, 1943 to Block #6.

In August 1943 Sgt. John Boyd, a radio operator and gunner from a B-25, was released into Block #3. He brought encouraging and reliable news that the Allied forces had stopped the Japanese in India and were in the process of pushing them back towards Burma. Sgt. Boyd said that he was on an experimental bombing mission when he was shot down.

The B-25 planes had been operating and dropping bombs on a dam in the Irrawaddy River from altitudes of 10,000 feet. After repeated bombings, reconnaissance planes reported the dam intact. A flight of three planes was assigned to skip-bomb and destroy the dam. The planes attacked one at a time. They approached at 1,500 feet and dropped to tree level height to release their bombs.

Sgt. Boyd's plane was the last in line and was hit by anti-aircraft, the Pilot used the speed of the plane to get some height but only Sgt. Boyd was successful in leaving the plane and using his parachute.

A Japanese interrogator told him that the dam had been destroyed many times and bamboo was used to make it look repaired. It was essentially being used as bait to entice the Allies to waste resources and become easy targets for anti-aircraft.

I was still required to work in the garden , however the crop we were growing had changed from eggplant to an edible and nutritious weed. The person who was responsible for this giant improvement in our diet was the Governor of the Andaman Islands. He and seven members of his staff were incarcerated in Block #3 while waiting to be repatriated. On his way to the latrine he saw a very small plant which he recognized as a weed that was eaten by natives in the Andaman Islands. He carefully retrieved it, planted it in a tin can and nurtured it until it came to seed. Brig. Hobson convinced the Japanese that it was worth trying as a substitute for the eggplants. They were delighted with the end product and as a result, we were growing "spinach" instead of eggplant. My food was now almost like a meal I sometimes had in New Orleans, red beans and rice, pork chops and spinach. The only difference was there wasn't any red beans or pork chops.

From June 1942 to April 1944 the Japanese commandant of the prison was Capt. Notozo Mitzumi. I don't know if he was consciously brutal to the prisoners or forced by necessity to limit food and medicine. It's hard to believe that a sane person would act as he did on September, 1943. A burning plane crash landed and six people got out of the plane alive. When the pilot, who was not injured, and five men with serious burns reached Rangoon Prison, Capt. Mitzumi ordered the guards to put them in solitary confinement. We learned of their condition and suffering the next day through the Chinese who delivered food to Block #5. They reported to Gen. Chi and he had a way of reaching us through the Gurkha compound.

Brig. Hobson immediately started efforts to get them moved into our Block so that even without medicine we might be able to do something to alleviate their pain. A whole day and night went by before his request was granted. As soon as Major Loring learned that we were going to receive some of the men, he told me that the seven American prisoners in Block #3 were relieved of all duty so that we could provide around-the-clock attention to the injured men. Three men were to be moved into Block #3 and two men were to be moved into Block #6. I thanked him and asked Lt. Wilson to try to find the rest of our crew. Sgt. Cummings was out on a work party. The rest of us, with the help of Sgt. Jock Ferrier prepared the room to receive them.

Sgt. Jock Ferrier was in charge of the area that had been designated as our hospital. Lieut. Hopes, Lieut. Jordan and Sgt. Daley were transferred to our compound. They had been several days without treatment. The first job we jointly attacked was to remove the maggots from the two most seriously injured men. Sgt. Maloc and Sgt.

Gonsalvez worked on Lieut. Jordan. Sgt. Ferrier helped me attend to Lieut. Hopes. Pvt. Radcliff tried to comfort Sgt. Daley who had burns on the back of one knee and on the back of his hands. The eye sockets of Lieutenants Jordan and Hopes were filled with maggots and maggots were in their ears. I don't know whether or not they were conscious but they pleaded for someone to stop sticking them in their ears. Major Loring procured and installed mosquito netting over them. It took quite a while to remove the maggots because more kept appearing. I realize that absent skilled professionals, medicine and narcotics there was little we could do to alleviate their suffering.

The realization that the Japanese had not provided that kind of treatment was appalling. The fact that they were put in solitary confinement was incomprehensible.

Lt .Wilson worked out a schedule that he would administer which did not include himself. There were two doctors in Block #3. One was Col. Mackenzie and the other was Major McCloud. Col. Mackenzie went to Block #6 to help treat the two men they received. In any case, Maj. McCloud conducted "sick call" every morning to determine who was to be excused from work parties. When he finished Sgt. Ferrier and I helped Sgt. Daley to where he was. I removed the bandage from his knee and a handful of maggots fell to the ground. Maj. McCloud told me that the maggots had cleaned out the wound and if we could keep it clean it would probably start healing. I then asked if a person in the condition of Lieut. Jordan could live.

Maj. McCloud said,"Jack, he is blind, deaf and his

fingers are falling off from gangrene. Would he want to?"

During the morning Lieut. Hopes died and mosquito netting had been moved to cover Sgt. Daley. I was scheduled to be on duty from 8 to 12 pm. About 10 o'clock I was seated side by side on the bench with Sgt. Ferrier. Lieut. Jordan had been restless and he suddenly succeeded on getting on his feet. He stood there with his arms flailing. I grabbed him and wrestled him down.

We discussed whether we should immobilize him.

Sgt. Ferrier said, "With what ?"

When we returned to our bench I said, "Major McCloud told me this morning that Jordan probably won't live and, if given a choice, he wouldn't want to live."

Sergeant Ferrier responded,"I agree. The best thing that could happen right now is for him to die."

Instead of responding to that statement. I simply said,"I understand you have a dagger that you use to make sure that the people we prepare for burial are really dead."

Sgt. Ferrier answered,"Yes, ever since Moore started moving after we prepared him for burial we have stuck a dagger into the corpse."

I said, "Get the dagger."

He went to his bed and came back holding the dagger.

He said, "I'll do it Lt. Horner."

He lifted the mosquito netting and dropped it behind him.

After what seemed an incredibly long time he lifted the netting and said,"I cannot do it."

I reached out my hand and he gave me the dagger. I knew at that moment that I was going to kill Jordan and I was comfortable with the idea.

I lifted the netting over my head and dropped it behind me. As it fell to the ground my resolve went with it. I berated myself. I cursed myself. I told myself he wants to die. I returned to the bench and gave the dagger to Sgt. Ferrier. Nothing was said between us, but I realized I lacked the mental fortitude to kill Jordan and I started crying.

Lieut. Jordan lived for another 48 hours.

16 FRIENDLY FIRE

We Americans still had one patient remaining. Sgt. Daley was responding to what little treatment we could offer. He was bedridden and needed help for calls of nature, together with having trouble recovering from the trauma he had experienced. Lt. Wilson adjusted the schedule so that during the day Sgt. Boyd and the hospital staff would take care of Daley and Sgt. Maloc and I would attend to him at night. Three days after Jordan's death, September 29, 1943, I was sitting inside the mosquito netting by Daley's bed when I heard the air raid alarm. He was frightened to death and he immediately wrapped his arms around my arm. A few moments later, Sgt. Maloc appeared and said he was ready to relieve me. I called to his attention it was not yet 12 o'clock.

He said, "I know that. I don't mind relieving you

early Lieutenant"

I knew both of us were supposed to be at the end of the slit trench during air raids, yet I didn't want to leave Daley alone.

I said,"I appreciate your offer, Sergent, but this guy has a stranglehold on me. I 'll stay. You better get out to the trench."

After a few minutes I heard a tremendous roar of approaching bombs that struck on each side of the building. Daley's bed was located in front of a window. The blast and shrapnel from the bomb came through the window. We had crouched below the bars and were not hit.

The experience of being on the receiving end of a bomb was over in a fraction of a second, nevertheless Daley was hysterical with fear. With considerable effort I uncoiled his arms so I could assess the damage and participate if any rescue work was necessary. Pvt. Radcliff came through the door leading to the latrines and asked if I knew where Sgt. Maloc was. I told him I didn't.

He shouted, "Well, I do !"

I followed him out of the door and saw that the second bomb had destroyed the latrine area and had buried our slit trench with hundreds of pounds of earth.

Everyone was digging frantically to try to uncover the trapped men. I joined them and quickly realized we had a monumental task. The slit trench had been covered with corrugated iron roofing which was now scrambled on top of the trench and then covered with earth. We could find one end of a piece of metal and, as we tried to lift it, we found that half of it was covered by another piece of roofing covered in earth. Eventually someone said to me that I couldn't help there and Daley needed me.

I returned inside and after a while they started to bring in, and lay out, the 13 that had been killed. I heard someone say that they were bringing in Sgt. Cummings. I went to where he was laying and for whatever reason I reached down and touched him. He was warm and I turned him over in preparation of giving resuscitation.

Col. McKenzie was there and he asked me, "What the hell are you doing?"

I said, "I'm going to do CPR."

He said, "God damn it, the man is dead and you're in my way !"

I have never forgiven Col. Mc Kenzie, or myself for listening to him.

Several days later a BOR said to me, "I'm sorry that Harold Cummings wasn't saved. Right after the explosion I heard him say 'Don't move I'm right under you' and then I passed out."

The same night that we lost 13 men a bomb fell in the Gurkha compound and killed 27 men.

The loss of Maloc, Cummings and Gonsalvez was traumatic, but there was no time to mourn. As grief stricken as George, Smith and I were we still had to take care of Sgt. Daley. Because I had spent so much time in the "infirmary" I became familiar with several of the sick and dying. One person was a man named Abramson that had helped Sgt. Ferrier administer to the sick until he developed Beri Beri. I decided to give him one of my eggs. I knelt down on the floor next to him.

After responding to his cheerful greeting, I said, "I don't know your first name, Sgt. Abramson."

He said, "It's Jeffrey, Sir, but my mother always called me "Jeffy."

I said, "That's a nice first name, but I like your nickname even better. Jeffy, I have a present for you."

I showed him the egg.

He said, "Oh, thank you Mr. Horner. But don't waste an egg on me. I'm not going to make it. Give the egg to someone who has a chance."

It took me a few moments to control my emotions and then I asked, "Who would you like to have the egg?"

"Give it to Private Simmons," Jeffy replied, "He's a healthy lad and will probably make it."

I approached Simmons and told him about Abramson's gift. He took the egg and shouted, "Thank you Jeffrey!"

Simmons had been wounded in the leg by shrapnel. His leg was very swollen and he said that the doctors hadn't been able to probe for the shrapnel because they didn't have any instruments. He understood that Brig. Hobson had requested from the Japanese the tools the doctors would need to probe.

Daley had received severe burns on the top of his hands, so he couldn't close them to feed himself or wipe his ass. He also got hysterical when he heard the air raid sirens. Since we had no bandages we kept him under the mosquito netting to keep the flies from infecting his burns.

When I reported for my shift I was told by Sgt. Ferrier

that instead of supplying medical tools the Japs had taken Simmons away. I said that I don't think we'll ever see Simmons again and Ferrier said he thought I was right.

Sometimes a very minor course of action can make a difference between success and failure. Also an insignificant decision might make the difference between life and death. If I had not decided to let the Burmese woman dry my shirt the day I was captured I would have been executed. After a couple of weeks had passed Sgt. Ferrier asked me to stop by his quarters when I had a chance. He showed me a beautiful pair of boots that had belonged to Lieut. Hopes.

He said, "I think you should have these."

I should have declined to take them by calling to his attention the fact that I had shoes and someone in the compound needed footwear far more than I did. Still, they were exceptional boots. I wanted them and I could always give my shoes away. I tried them on and they fit perfectly. I wore the boots later when I took out a funeral party.

I had been a prisoner nearly a year and routine relations between the guards and prisoners had mellowed somewhat. Burial parties were treated with considerable respect. Even though most prisoners wore only a fundoshi (Japanese underwear similar to a loin cloth) during the day, burial parties were fully dressed in borrowed, if needed, pants, shirts and shoes. The burial ceremony consisted of slow marching out of the compound and marching through the front gate to an open truck. We were then transported a short distance to the cemetery.

At the cemetery, we walked a good distance to a grave

that had been dug by coolies. After the body was dropped as gently as possible into the hole, I was permitted to read John 11:25 from a small Bible. I read aloud, *"I am the resurrection and the life. He who believes in me live, even though he dies, and whoever lives by believing in me shall never die "*

By the time we returned to Block #3 I felt I had worn the boots long enough to establish they were a good fit and I gave away my shoes. This occurred in November 1943 and I seldom wore the boots until April 29, 1945. Like most of the prisoners I went barefoot or, on occasions when the latrine was exceptionally dirty, wore homemade wood clogs. Switching my footwear was an almost fatal mistake as you will learn later in my story.

November 30, 1943 - New Orleans Louisiana.

An article in the Monroe, Louisiana Liberal reports that Sergeant Cummings was killed on September 29th. From other newspaper articles, he learns that Sergeants Maloc and Gonsalvez were killed the same day. My father now knows that of the six people that parachuted from the B-17, Smith Radcliffe and George Wilson were alive and prisoners of war. His son was still MIA.

He realized there was a lot of evidence that I never became a prisoner of war. Of course, there was still a remote chance that I survived and was hiding in some remote native village.

He wanted to believe, but he could not convince himself.

He decided to keep his conclusions to himself and nurture my mother's faith.

My mother continued to pray.

SERGT. CUMMINGS' DEATH REPORTED

Police Officer and Mrs. M. W. Cummings, 3112 Lee avenue, have just been informed by the war department at Washington, D. C., that their son, Sergeant Harold B. Cummings, who had been captured by the Japanese in Burma and held prisoner for many months, had died last November 29.

He was a graduate of Ouachita Parish High school and enlisted September 9, 1939.

He had been awarded a silver star for gallantry.

Besides his parents, Sergeant Cummings leaves a brother, Corporal Eldrea Cummings, who is taking pilot training in a college in Cleveland, O.; and a sister, Mrs. Hazel Little, Orange, Tex.

17 THE BRITISH

These events I have recorded occurred during the first year that I was in Block #3. During that time I became very friendly with the British officers. Very few were professional soldiers but some of them had been living in India and Burma for years. They represented major British companies involved in shipping, importing and exporting, agricultural interests (growing tea leaves and rice). They were all a part of the restricted community of people that had access to country clubs (gymkhanas) which Indians and Burmese were not permitted to join. The progeny of mixed marriages were called Chichi and were considered inferior to the British nationals. I mention this because the British had a criterion for determining ones position in society. I admired the way they adjusted to the deprivations of prison life after having been so privileged.

While it was unpleasant for all of us, it was particularly difficult for some of the injured. One officer had been shot through his mouth and when it healed his mouth extended halfway to his ear. He had to hold his cheek together with his fingers so that he could eat. When I first met Capt. Toothill it was distasteful to look at him and I had to force myself to be nonchalant. If he could endure his injury I had to ignore it. One uninhibited and jovial officer had received shrapnel through the foreskin of his penis. If anyone was interested, and even if they weren't, he would pinch the end of his foreskin and urinate in four or five different directions. A young Irishman had a broken wrist which healed without having been set. His hand was cockeyed to his arm and he was constantly in fear of breaking it again.

The young officers had either enlisted or were recruited from universities. Since names like Oxford and Cambridge kept popping up, I came to the conclusion that they were from wealthy families. Nevertheless, they, like the rest of us, grew accustomed to the conditions under which we lived. With so much time on our hands conversation became the primary form of entertainment. One man had an inexhaustible repertoire of jokes. It seems that everyone had unique and interesting experiences from both before and during war. I must admit I was surprised at the number of ghost stories, purporting to be real, that were told by Capt. Colgan of the Inniskillin Fusilier's. They were long, very well told and interesting. A lot of spice was added because he insisted they were true.

I think one of the most interesting stories was told by the manager of a tea farm. His story also shows the relationship of the white man with the natives of South Asia. After having spent four years in India and having exhausted the possibility of finding an English girlfriend or wife, he decided to acquire one from Nepal. It was standard practice for Nepalese parents of a teenage girl to offer to swap, for a period of time, their daughter for a cash settlement. Eventually, when the purchaser returned to England, the girl would return to Nepal. Native marriage counselors carefully scrutinized the purchaser and the purchaser had a chance to meet and analyze his purchase.

Capt. Charles Nutter, the tea planter, was delighted with his purchase. They lived very much like a wealthy husband and wife except that he could not take her to the available country club. To have some sort of a social life there was considerable visiting amongst men who had acquired native "wives". He talked at length about their loving relationship and their passionate sex life. I might mention here that food was a far more popular subject than sex. In any case, Charles was concerned because he had sent her back, with considerable funds, to her parents. He said he now realized how much she meant to him and wished he had made other arrangements.

I became very friendly with Capt. Marshall Foster. He was a few years older than me and considerably more mature. He grew up exposed and comfortable with social protocol that I barely understood. His mother had been a debutante and his father a wealthy barrister. When he finished public (English for private) school, he accepted a position in India with a major ship line. Being a junior executive of a major ship line was an enviable position for a young man. They had minor tasks and responsibilities, and were a major part of the social life of the expatriate British community.

The main representative of a British company was known as Number One. The normal career path was that, after 10 or 15 years, a Number One returned home as a senior executive. While serving in India the household staff of a Number One consisted of full-time cooks, maids, gardeners and, if necessary, nannies. They enjoyed a very active social life in the tight knit British, European and American community. Marshall had reached the Number Two position before he joined the Army.

My background was the opposite of his. My parents couldn't teach me anything about high society, still I am eternally grateful for what they did teach me. From them I learned the importance of being truthful, honest, and having good table manners. I guess I manage to cope somehow, yet even today I would rather dig ditches than go to a cocktail party. I'm generally at a loss as to what to say and, when I try, say the wrong thing.

Capt. Foster was in command of a Gurkha regiment during the battle at the oil fields. A successful retreat meant they had to cross a river. The Gurkhas came from Nepal and had never seen a body of water big enough to swim in. They faced a choice of drowning or being killed by mortar and rifle fire. After a spirited but useless defense, Marshall surrendered and was taken prisoner. His troops were in Block #2. The Gurkhas are mercenaries who have made a career of fighting for the British and returning to their native Nepal with honor and pensions. They are notorious for fierceness, obedience and dedication to duty. Their officers were always British nationals who communicated with them using Hindi-Urdu which was the lingua franca for all of India. At the colloquial level the two languages are indistinguishable and easy to learn.

One evening a discussion between Marshall and me wandered into religion. I told him that in New Orleans there was no religious prejudice or intolerance. Of course, segregation existed based on race and Negros were not treated as equals. The Jim Crow laws of the South were much harsher than treatment accorded the Indians by the British. New Orleans is primarily Roman Catholic and I attended the Jesuit University, Loyola. Every year Loyola offered a scholastic scholarship to the valedictorian of my public high school. The winner the year I graduated was a Jewish boy who accepted the scholarship. Although all Catholics at Loyola were required to take a course in religion, he was excused from the requirement. The University did not discriminate against Jews or Protestants in any way.

I quit school after my sophomore year and joined a traveling sales group that sold magazine subscriptions. My sales training consisted of instructions to say, "I'm working my way through Loyola University" and then ask the mark to subscribe to a magazine. Our first stop was in Houston Texas which is in the heart of the Bible Belt.

When I finished my opening statement the woman said, "Why don't you go sell your magazines to those Catholics in New Orleans?" She then slammed the door. It was the first time I actually encountered religious intolerance, I overcame my problem by substituting Tulane for Loyola.

Marshall said, "Jack, Scots are still fighting the Battle

of Culloden which occurred in 1689. If we had met in Scotland and had become good friends and someone told me you were a papist, I would never have talked to you again. I would have acted that way because of peer pressure. In Bombay I realized that you papist aren't a bad lot. I frequently played badminton with a priest."

My Army records show that I am a Catholic and his records show him to be a Presbyterian, it was still easy for us to agree that religion has been more of a problem than a boon to humanity. Marshall mentioned that I was attending the clandestine religious services on Yatsuma days and he wondered why. I told him the meetings were non-denominational and the attendees received a lot of solace and comfort. Since the Japanese had forbidden us to have religious meetings I felt like I should support the group. The worst that could happen is that I would be slapped a bit and put in solitary for a short while.

Marshall said jokingly, "Then you don't believe that Jesus loves you."

I answered, "I can't believe in a Supreme Being when I see what is happening here. If there is one, He certainly doesn't have the attributes priests and ministers have given him. Like mercy for one thing. And I feel that He hasn't '*leadeth me beside still waters*', He leadeth me into this crock of shit!"

Marshall said, "Based on your absolutely ridiculous reasoning, I'll start attending prayer meetings with you."

As time went on, fewer and fewer prisoners attended the meetings and Marshall and I stopped going.

18 ROOM & BOARD

At the end of a year it was obvious that George was not coping as well as me. Everyone in the compound received the same amount of food except, of course, the cooks. After just a casual glance you could tell they were not going hungry. Some of the senior officers had money to buy extra food, tobacco and soap. As I have said before, officers were treated better than enlisted men.

In accordance with the Geneva Convention, officers were paid according to rank. As a Second Lieutenant I received 90 Japanese dollars a month. Eighty five dollars was deducted for room and board and, I was informed, that I was investing four dollars a month in Japanese war bonds.

A Burmese vendor was allowed into the compound once a month. Since he dealt in rupees the rate of exchange was three rupees to one dollar. George and I had agreed to pool our resources and to share with our crew the extras we could purchase. One rupee could buy either three hard-boiled eggs, 12 cheroots or a small slab of jaggery (solidified molasses). The amount of food we purchased was of insignificant nutritional value, however it added a little flavor to the rice. We crushed the cheroots to get tobacco for our pipes. I was told that work parties were paid ten cents a day for each BOR and 15 cents for each noncommissioned officer. It appeared to be true because the guards were very meticulous when filling out a report that was ostensibly for their bookkeeping. I remember being in charge of a work party that had very few NCOs. When asked for the number I simply said, "Roman Catholics hold up your hands."

Individual BOR did not receive any money but I understood that the compound received extra food purchased with the money earned by the work parties. At times George, despite his protest, received extra eggs from our pooled resources but there was no other way to supplement his rations.

It was during this time that my skin turned bright yellow. After Tenko I sought the advice of Major McCloud. He said I had hepatitis. He also said that there were three different kinds of the disease and he had no way to treat them. According to the Major there were no other cases of jaundice in the compound and my skin would clear up in two or three days. There is a popular saying that "misery loves company". I can confirm that it's true. I was doing reasonably well sharing diarrhea, jungle soars and hunger with over 150 other men, yet I was very upset at having hepatitis alone. Since I didn't feel weak or sick or have any pain, life went on as usual. After a few days, when the yellow disappeared, I felt like I had won a lottery.

The Japanese were now publishing an English

language newspaper which, in addition to supposition and rumor, was our source of information. During the year books began to be circulated amongst the prisoners. The assumption was that they were smuggled in by the work parties. It was alittle difficult to believe that they were being brought in without the guards seeing them because of the large size of the books and the large number that were in the compound. Of course, there was no library system, books were simply passed from person to person until they actually met their demise as toilet paper.

The first book I read was "Pride And Prejudice", soon after that I read HG Wells "Outline of History", the "Forsyte Saga", "Hamlet", "Macbeth", and dozens of other books. I think "Origin of the Species" by Charles Darwin was the most interesting book that I ever read. It was a copy of the document he submitted to the Royal Society of Britain to support his theory of evolution. I had first heard the title "Origin of the Species" in 1930 when I was attending catechism classes in preparation for my Confirmation. At that time I was instructed that it was a venial sin to read books on the "Prohibited Reading List". "Origins" was on the list. The book explained how fauna and flora have evolved over millions of years, how a species, struggling to survive, is changed by geography, climate, cross breeding, domestication and heredity.

As I read I was seated, leaning against the four-inch teak bars that enclosed my cell. I suddenly felt a bedbug bite me. He left a row of three painful welts. I caught and mashed him. He retaliated by emitting a terrible, stinking odor. Block #3 was infested with bedbugs and this encounter was typical. I knew nothing about the bed bugs' diet, love life or struggle for existence, but I knew the varmint was the result of evolution. On the other hand, according to Colossians 1:16, God is the creator of all things: good and evil. If that were true, a benevolent Creator, wanting the best for Man, would never have created a stinking blood-sucking bed bug.

The Japanese English newspaper was always referred to as the "bloody mucus". It was difficult to discount the newspaper's version of the Battle for Burma. The work parties brought in rumors that seemed to validate the newspapers articles.

A persistent rumor was that Gen."Vinegar"Joe Stillwell predicted he would be in Rangoon by Christmas. I noticed that the rumor did not say which year. United States Air Force personnel began arriving at the prison in the middle of 1943, and I can't remember them bringing much news of the CBI Theatre of Operation. The Battle for Burma was under the command of British General Slim.

Despite the fact that the United States was providing air support there were no ground troops until General Stillwell formed a task force, named Merrill's Marauders. Their success operating behind enemy lines apparently fueled "Vinegar Joe's" optimism, yet neither he nor any of them, even as prisoners, ever reached Rangoon.

A British group of guerrillas known as Wingate's Raiders was active in 1943. They were very successful ,still, some of the sick and wounded men were captured and incarcerated in Block #6. From them we learned that Myitkyina was still occupied by the Japanese. This was very disappointing because I had dropped bombs on Myitkyina in May of 1942. The one thing of which I was certain is that Allied troops would not be in Rangoon for Christmas.

B-24 planes continued to bomb Rangoon both day and night. It was a mixed blessing because I took it as a sign that we were winning the battle. Unfortunately, the pipes of the city water department were frequently broken and our supply of water was cut off. We did have a central pump house which could substitute for the city water system. Unfortunately the pumps were run by electricity and the electrical system of Rangoon suffered the same fate as the water department.

We could still get a limited amount of water for cooking and drinking by using a hand pump. Without water the sanitary condition of latrines became almost unbearable. Rangoon, under the British, was a very modern city and we were never without water more than a couple of days because the Water and Power Department continued to function.

19 CHRISTMAS '43

Christmas 1943 fell on a Friday. Marshall Foster decided that since Friday was a work day, we would celebrate Christmas on Sunday, December 28th. He asked Brig. Hobson to requests permission from the Japanese to gather for religious services and a program to entertain the Officers and British Other Ranks.

Brig. Hobson said, "If I ask for permission and it is denied I will forbid you to gather. If we go forward with your plans and are discovered by the Japanese, I will say I did not give you permission to gather nor did I know you were gathering. You and I would then be subjected to some sort of punishment."

Marshall asked, "What are the chances that they will approve of us meeting?"

Brig. Hobson answered, "I don't know, Marshall. The commandant is very unpredictable. I'll ask if you want me to or you can go ahead with your plans without the Commandant's permission."

Marshall asked Brig. Hobson, "Are you willing to risk

the punishment?"

Brigadier Hobson replied, "The punishments I've received this last year and a half have been more degrading than painful. I think what you are proposing will build morale. I'll ask for permission if you want me to."

Marshall replied, "Don't ask and thank you."
Immediately after talking to Brig. Hobson, Marshall found me and said, "Jack, I'm determined to make this Christmas a festive affair and I want you to help me."

Below is the conversation as I recall it,

Me, "If we get caught, who gets the shit slapped out of them, you or me?"

Marshall, "Me!"

Me, "Okay Marshall now that we have that settled, let me ask you a few questions. First thing is where are you going to do the show for 150 people without attracting attention?"

Marshall, "The performances will be in each room for the inmates of the room. The rest of the prisoners will be milling around outside as they usually do on Yatsuma days. The troupe will move from room to room and do five or possibly six performances."

Me, "I doubt if I can be of much help, but I'll do anything you ask me to do. Let me call to your attention that you don't have a band, costumes, acrobats or a chorus line.

Marshall, "Let's cross these bridges as we come to them. You're wrong about not having dancers. We have the "Ladies from Hell" if we can improvise a kilt. Tommy Dunn, our Irish Tenor will sing. Chris Morgan probably has a few jokes that he hasn't told. You can help me write a small skit for two or three of the men. There is also a BOR named "Shifty" Smith who says that before he joined the service he was a thief. He describes himself as an accomplished professional thief. The way this fellow describes the thefts are great stories and extremely funny. I think a story from him would add variety to the show. If needed, I would serve as Master of Ceremonies. It will all work out, Jack. The cooks have assured me that we will have a memorable Christmas dinner!"

Me, "How are they going to do that, Marshall?"

Marshall, "Everyone is going to receive two! Repeat two! Fried Rice Balls for Christmas dinner."

Marshall explained the cooks had been hoarding vegetable oil so that they could make Rice Balls. These were a treat that we received once every couple of months. I don't know if they were truly delicious or we just needed the oil and salt. Whenever we ate rice balls someone would invariably say he could make a living selling rice balls in Piccadilly Square.

Everyone involved was very enthusiastic. We had a week to prepare the program. Of course Dunn, Morgan, and Smith would work up their routine by themselves after Marshall decided how long they would perform. The Cameroonians who volunteered to do the dancing said they would improvise their own kilts. They would dance alone and perform two dances. Burns would do a Highland Jig followed by McCabe doing a Highland Fling. Later in the program Burns would do a Highland Fling and McCabe would do the Highland Jig. It was a revelation to me that these are real discernibly different dances. The Jig was done prior to going into battle. The Fling was done to celebrate a feast or party. The dancing is done over two crossed swords and I was given the relatively easy task of providing them (out of wood of course).

We had very little paper so the skit that Marshall wrote was skeletal to say the least. It had to do with a bloke (Pvt. Johnson) trying to pick up a broad (Cpl. Parkins). The two of them are seated some distance apart facing a bartender (Chris Morgan) who faces them with his back to the audience. Slowly, after considerable repartee, Johnson moves from stool to stool until they are seated together. He then put his arm around Parkins and tweaks her breast. Johnson presses her breast with his hand and she puts her hand over his and smiles.

A late arrival (Shifty Smith), comes through the door and ask,"Anyone for darts?"

Johnson immediately leaves Parkins and says, "Count me in, lad!"

I thought the skit was pretty weak but I was unconcerned until Marshall said,"Jack, you will serve as director and stage hand."

I protested,"Wait a minute Marshall, there's no dialogue."

Marshall replied, "The actors will work out the dialogue. You monitor the continuity and the acting."

I was puzzled as to exactly what my role would be until the actors worked out the opening repartee. I suggested that they do this script exactly as they intend to Christmas Day.

They conferred amongst themselves.

I said, "Lights! Camera! Action!"

It took them about 30 seconds to stumble through their lines. I told them that they did very good and our goal, as we went forward, was either to remember the lines perfectly or to be able to ad-lib fluently.

I mention to Parkins that in an attempt to talk like a woman he was lisping like a "queer".

Johnson immediately said, "If he's queer, I'm not going to touch his breast!"

We all chuckled a bit. Parkins then spoke a couple lines in a higher pitch and we all agreed he definitely didn't sound like a man. He agreed to use his stage voice as much as possible to perfect it. I concluded that actors can't perform and, at the same time, judge the quality of their work. I could, as a director, help them improve their acting. I now felt I could do the job I had been given by Marshall.

Since I became a POW I often thought of my parents even though there was little stimuli to foster such thoughts. When Tom Dunn told me that the songs he proposed to sing included "I'll take you home again, Kathleen" I was transported back to my childhood. I could see my mother and father embracing. The song was popular just before World War I when my father was courting my mother. It must have been their favorite piece of music then because it was frequently played on our phonograph. I felt a real connection to them and I savored the moment.

Marshall was determined that we would produce the following program and perform it without a hitch.

1. Marshall - MC - Greetings and Intro of acts   2.0 min
2. Chris Morgan - Comic   5.0 min
3. Burns - Dancer Irish Jig   0.5 min
4. McCabe - Dancer Fling   0.5 min
5. Burns - Dancer Fling   0.5 min
6. McCabe - Dancer Irish Jig   0.5 min
7. Dunn - Singer -"Danny Boy"
          "An Irish Lullaby "   2.5 min
8. Smith - Thief - Tales of his profession   5.0 min
9.,10.,11.,12. - Repeat Dancers (4 x 0.5)   2.0 min
13. Dunn - Singer -
     "I'll take you home again Kathleen"   2.0 min
14. Johnson, Parkins, Morgan and Smith - Skit   5.0 min
15. Marshall - MC - Closes show   1.0 min

I was pleased to see that the time allocated for each act was reasonable and the program would last 25 minutes. Rehearsals for the skit went extremely well. The four actors were creative and very witty. The dialogue also developed so naturally that it was easy to remember.

I helped a great deal by not saying anything. I did however make small contributions like having the bartender move to the end of the bar and turn to deliver his lines so that the audience could hear them. Major Loring loaned me his watch so that I could time some of the dialogue. I discovered that it takes a lot of conversation to use up five minutes.

Since time and tide wait for no man, Christmas finally came. I sat in the first row and watched Marshall greet the audience and introduce Chris Morgan. Chris was at his best. His jokes were very funny and told in the context of being events and occurrences in his life. The audience was obviously very well entertained. In fact his monologue lasted over six minutes because he had to stop speaking until the laughter died. Marshall gave me a "thumbs up"and introduced the dancers.

I had never seen a Scottish Dancer, I had seen pictures of Scotsman in kilts. When Burns started to dance my imagination took hold. As he danced, his improvised dress looked like a kilt. It flared as he put one bent leg over the other and moved about the swords. He started with his hands on his hips still there was also a lot of upper body movements. I could even hear the Scottish bagpipes as he danced. Burns only danced for about 30 seconds yet it was beautiful. He and McCabe did four dances and they were very well received. As Marshall was introducing Tommy Dunn, Major Loring told me through the bars that the applause was too loud.

Marshall announced,"Before Tommy sings I want to do a survey. How many NCOs are in the audience?" Four people held up their hands. Marshall then instructed all Roman Catholics hold up their hands.

He then announced, "Your applause has been too loud and might attract attention that we don't want. For the rest of the show only NCOs, Roman Catholics, women and children have permission to applaud. And now, here is one of the finest tenors in the British Army, Tommy Dunn."

He, of course, sang *a cappella,* yet I could hear the music and it was beautiful. The applause was much reduced in volume because we didn't have many women

MIA: Missing In Action   107

and children. Marshall then introduced "Shifty" Smith. I am certain that he had briefed Marshall on his routine but he had not shared the contents with anyone. Before he joined the Army, Smith was a thief. He described how he and his friends stole the lead roof off of a building while people inside were gambling. It required him to visit the gamblers and advise them that he was doing remodeling work next door and he hoped he would not disturb them. He related the conversations between him and his fellow thieves and the frequent trips to assure the gamblers that he wouldn't be too much longer. He knew his interruptions annoyed the gamblers so he made a special trip to apologize for disturbing them. He was interesting and funny and the audience roared with laughter. Burns and McCabe danced again and Tommy Dunn sang "I'll take you home again Kathleen".

After the applause Marshall and I set up the props which consisted of a long board which served as the bar and two stools for Johnson and Parkins. It's very difficult without makeup to make a man like Parkins look like a girl, but we tried. Marshall assured everyone that regardless of appearances Parkins was a girl and Johnson was horny. With that the actors took their positions and the skit started. Speaking as the (ahem) director I was very pleased and the audience was ecstatic.

We did two more shows before dinner and two after. The Christmas dinner was a tremendous success. While it would not compare favorably with a traditional turkey dinner it was exceptional when we received two rice balls.

20 TO KILL OR NOT TO KILL?

Two or three days after Christmas, I mentioned to Marshall that I was having a recurring nightmare. Ever since Lieut. Jordan died I occasionally dreamt I was trying to hold him down and he fought me with his gangrenous hands and his burned head. I also confided that I could not get rid of a feeling of guilt because I had not stopped his pain by killing him.

Marshall said, "Don't be so hard on yourself, Jack, you behaved exactly the way I would have."

I said, "If I had killed Jordan, how many people in this compound would have disapproved."

Marshall responded, "I don't think anyone would have ever known, and if they did, at least 99% would have approved of you doing it and very few, if any, would have done it themselves. You see, Jack, we are all a product of our religious training. Moses said *"thou shall not kill"* and we all accept that as a commandment that we can't violate. If I am right about the 99%, then obviously the right thing would have been to kill him."

I thought a while and then confessed, "That is what troubles me so much, Marshall, I know what I should've done. What haunts me is I didn't have the guts to do it.

Marshall said, "Let me say again, forget it and don't be so hard on yourself."

I felt a lot better after talking to Marshall and I had fewer nightmares.

I spent a considerable amount of time trying to grasp the concept of right and wrong with which I had been confronted. Despite the fact that I had not done the right thing, everyone thought that my behavior was normal.

My thoughts turned to the Japanese commandant, Capt. Mitzumi, and the people who handled the airmen on their way to Rangoon. They did not have the facilities or medication to handle the victims, however, if they had killed them they would have been condemned as diabolical monsters. War creates its own set of rules depending on where and when the action takes place. On the battlefield the opponents are committed to killing each other but immediately after the engagement, the victors are expected to supply medical care and transportation to their defeated, wounded opponents.

It doesn't happen.

The victors are now saddled with prisoners that are a mixture of tired, sick and wounded. This is why "death marches" occur. If prisoners that fell down were allowed to live, they might recover and become combatants again.

I decided that distinguishing right from wrong during a war was a conundrum. Of course the relationship between captured soldiers and their captors varies dramatically from immediately after combat to long-term incarceration.

21 CONSORTING WITH THE ENEMY

Except for the Burmese Home Guard soldiers I had been treated reasonably well until I met Weno. Unlike the other guards, he seemed sadistic when he punished prisoners for what he perceived as a violation of a rule or a failure to properly salute. Most of the guards seemed indifferent to the inmates as long as they were saluted properly. Some of them, however, had duties that required them to spend long boring hours with the prisoners. I don't know if friendship might have developed between Kuma and I if we had been able to communicate with each other.

After the shot put contest, the garden work party engaged in several athletic activities. We did standing high jump, standing broad jump and javelin throw (with bamboo). We never had a ball of any kind, but we had a pretty hefty round flat rock that we threw as a discus.

When I participated in any of these events, Kuma would act like my cheering section by shouting out "Hawn-uh" every now and then. I know that on the day we were bombed at the front gate, he feared there may be immediate repercussions and he sent me back to Block #3.

Work parties which consisted of one officer and 10 to 20 enlisted personnel were sent out daily to sites where they were needed. The guards seldom stayed with the workforce after it was delivered to the work site. The Japanese Project Manager assigned the task to be done and there was very little disciplinary action and no security.

Of course everyone knew that there was absolutely no chance of a Caucasian escaping and making his way back to friendly territory. Some of these jobs were repetitive and the Japanese became familiar with some of the prisoners. During rest breaks, the Japanese asked questions using sign language about Britain, the United States and baseball. Food was occasionally given to the work parties.

Among the senior British NCO's was a man named Sollenberg. He was the son of a British soldier who had a Chichi wife. The wife was the offspring of a Frenchman and a Hindu. In New Orleans dogs of several mixed breeds are called "cayoodles". They make great pets and are unusually smart. Nathan Sollenberg was a human cayoodle with extraordinary linguistic ability. His army career had taken him to China where he learned some Mandarin in addition to English, French, Hindustani and Urdu. While most prisoners had difficulty learning how to count to 10 in Japanese and learn some required commands, Nathan quickly acquired a large vocabulary.

The Japanese interpreter, who we called "Goggles" for obvious reasons, engaged Nathan in conversations for the purpose of improving his English. Nathan, of course, used Goggles to improve his Japanese. On work parties the fact that he spoke a little Japanese frequently led to extended conversations using sign language, Japanese and English.

After a year in prison Nathan could speak simple conversational Japanese. There's no question that some of the guards liked Nathan. I think the ultimate proof was when, after the evening meal, Nathan was taken away. He was returned a couple of hours later by three laughing and giggling guards. Two of them were supporting an obviously intoxicated and wobbly Nathan. He was very happy. I suspect the guards were happy too.

22 NO NEWS IS TOUGH

On January 4, 1944   I had just passed my 25th birthday and had been a prisoner for one year and seven months. During that time I had not learned any reliable information about the progress of the war. I knew on June 4, 1942 that, less than six months after Pearl Harbor, enough Navy Vessels had been repaired to engage the Japanese fleet. In the Battle of the Coral Sea we defeated the Japanese and kept them from invading Australia. In Europe there was only an Eastern Front and the Russians were retreating. In North Africa Germany's General Rommel was threatening Alexandria and the Suez Canal.

In the CBI Theatre of Operations the British had retreated from Burma to India.   Although Doolittle's raid on Tokyo was a morale builder, it was not tactically important. The flying Tigers under Gen. Claire Chennault had retreated from China. My B-17 was the last 10th Air Force plane capable of bombing Rangoon. An objective analysis of the information I had when I was shot down would indicate that the Allies were losing the war.

During 1942 and 1943 I never received any reliable information that was very encouraging. I let myself succumb to the sanguine rumors from time to time, but I knew they were inaccurate. The only concrete evidence we had that the Allies were still waging war in Burma were the frequent raids by the B-24's which had replaced the B-17's. It is hard to imagine how isolated a compound such as mine could be. Think of a small town without telephones or radio surrounded by an inhospitable forest.

In May of 1944 Rangoon prison got a new commandant. Unconfirmed rumors said that he was a Christian. In any case he decided that he wanted to rearrange the prisoners so that there would only be soldiers from Britain in Block #3. The rest of the soldiers which included Americans, Australians, New Zealanders and Rhodesians and all the very ill were moved to Block #6. Some survivors of Wingate's Raiders were moved from Block #6 to Block #3. The Japanese also delegated Major Nigel Loring to be the senior officer and ordered him to reorganize the compound so it would function like Block #3. Major Nigel Loring was the only British officer transferred to Block #6.

The main building in Block #6 was identical to the one in Block #3 The British Officers were in one of the large rooms the Americans were in the other. I was given a place on the floor next to the door. There was a great deal of handshaking, storytelling and camaraderie in our room. Most of my new roommates were survivors of planes that had been either shot down by Zeros or anti-aircraft. Although some had been captured after crash landing, the majority parachuted into captivity. One of the activities that the inmates shared was looking at photographs that most everyone carried in their wallets.

One of the men, Harold Goad, showed me a picture of his wife, Helen.

I mentioned that she was very attractive and he said, "Yes, she is. But I wonder what will happen if I get out of here alive. You see I forced her to agree that if I were killed she would not waste her life grieving but would go on living as if she had never met me. Until recently I've dreamed about the life we would enjoy if I survive and return home. I learned from some new arrivals from my squadron that I have been listed as killed in action. It bothers me a great deal to know that Helen thinks I'm dead."

I said, "I'm sure it does, Harold. Why were you reported KIA?"

Harold explained that his plane was hit and exploded ejecting him into space about 12,000 feet above ground. Believing that if he opened his parachute he would be a target for the Zeros, he delayed pulling the ripcord. When he did, the parachute opened, he swung once and hit the ground. Harold was the only survivor from his plane and no one saw his parachute open.

I didn't have a photograph to share because I lost my wallet and wrist watch a half hour after landing in Burma.

The conversation with Harold made me think of my fiancée, Betty. While I was in Block #3, amongst the British there was very little, if anything, to cause me to think of her. Now, I was very much at home with Americans who were generally my age and had similar backgrounds. I spent four months in Miami learning navigation and, whenever I had free time, I was with Betty. She was 18 years old and a beauty. We enjoyed fun and games and being together, however I don't think you would describe our relationship as "being in love."

After I left Miami I don't remember us communicating by letter or telephone. America declared war on Japan on December the eighth and I reached MacDill Air Force Base located in Tampa, Florida on Christmas Day. Before New Year's I joined Capt. Douglas Sharp's crew and we were dispatched to ferry our B-17 to Karachi. We were trying to reach Belem, Brazil when we encountered an equatorial front. Doug told me that we would have to land at one of the emergency airfields that were under construction. I had the coordinates. The field was about 100 miles from where we were. Our ETA (estimated time of arrival) and sunset were exactly the same.

I was holding my breath when Doug said,"Jack where's the airfield?"

I replied,"We should be right over it."

Doug practically screamed, "We are! We are! Put on your seat belts. We only have one chance at landing. By the time I reach the ground it will be dark." The plane hit the ground, bounced and then rolled 750 feet until the nose and propellers dug into the ground. No one was hurt and a few days later we were flown to Belem to await transportation back to the MacDill Base. It was almost a month before we returned to MacDill and another month before we received a new plane.

I don't know what possessed me to do it, nevertheless during this time I called Betty. She seemed delighted to hear from me and immediately made arrangements to come to Tampa for a long weekend. Capt. Sharp gave me permission to leave the base as long as he and personnel knew where I was. I made the necessary arrangements and Betty and I checked into the Floridian Hotel. There is no question in my mind that Betty and I liked each other a great deal and enjoyed being together. I don't think my feelings justified my actions, however, on the last day of her visit I proposed and gave her a diamond engagement ring. Now, unlike Harold, my main concern was that Elizabeth Defriese would be waiting to marry me. I knew that if I survived I wanted to tackle civilian life without any baggage whatsoever. I fervently hoped that Betty would be married.

One of my new cell mates, "Tex" Parrish, told me that he was forced to parachute when he lost power while flying the "Hump". When I told him I didn't have the faintest idea what he meant, he explained that he was flying cargo from India to Kuming, China. The Himalayas are a mountain range that separates India and Burma from China. They average over 20,000 feet high but just north of Myitkyina there is a group that is only 16,000 feet high.

When the Allies lost the use of the Burma Road they created an air cargo company to transport material to the nationalist in China. The relatively low peaks over which they flew was nicknamed the "Hump". According to Tex hundreds of planes delivered tons of war supplies. He said the typical trip took four hours going and, because of head winds, five hours returning. Tex was told the planes delivered far more supplies to Chiang Kai-shek than had ever been delivered via the Burma road. Generally speaking all the airmen in Block #6 were in excellent health.

In Block #3, I had been treated as the Senior American Officer. Brig. Hobson and Major Loring advised me that they would discipline the American prisoners, if necessary, through me. After two years of exposure I recognize that the British Senior Officers were, in addition to being experienced soldiers, experienced prisoners. I never had any reservations about approving their strategies. In Block #6 there were three officers who were senior to me. There were two pilots who were Majors and a Lieutenant Colonel who had been captured while serving as a liaison officer with the Chinese.

I remembered how I felt when Sgt. Maloc explained my responsibilities to me. I now felt that the Senior American Officers in Block #6 should and would act in my best interest to help me survive. I was surprised to learn that a British Air Force Officer had been in charge of the block instead of one of them. I was even more surprised when, after several days, Nigel Loring sought me out and said he wanted to talk to me.

I said, "Sure, Nigel, what about?"

He replied, "Your Senior Officers. I can't understand their reasoning but they don't approve of what I want to do."

I asked, "What do you want to do?"

Nigel did not answer my question.

Instead he stated, "Look, Jack, they disapprove of work parties for Americans. Work parties sent from this block are all British soldiers, no Americans."

I asked, "Do they realize that we get extra food because of the work parties?"

Nigel said, "I've explained that but they are adamant that they will not approve of Americans being assigned to work parties."

I explained to Nigel that none of the American Officers were going to disagree or oppose the Colonel because of his rank and the fact that he was a graduate of West Point. Nigel then told me that he intended to exclude the American Senior Officers from any strategic planning. He was going to consider me the Senior Officer and we would have the same relation we had in Block #3.

I told Nigel if that solved his problems it was okay by me.

Dateline May, June and July 1944

New Orleans Louisiana.

In May my father reads a newspaper article saying that the British have launched an offensive at Imphal, India and are pushing the Japanese back into Burma. He also is aware June 6 (two years after I was shot down) was D-Day in Europe. In July, United States forces under Gen. McArthur and Adm. Nimitz are on a relentless drive to mainland Japan. He recognizes that we are winning the war.

His health has suffered since he first learned I was missing in action and he can't force himself to rationalize that I am still alive.

My mother continues to pray.

23 MAKING A DIFFERENCE

A couple of days later Nigel asked me if I could make a plate out of the roofing material that was available. He described what he wanted as a 4"x 8" dish that would hold water but not have any areas that could not be cleaned and kept dry. We agreed that, although it wouldn't be easy, the plates were very much needed by some of the men. I embarked on my manufacturing career with 10 of the "walking sick". The raw material was 3' x 6' malleable corrugated iron. My toolbox consisted of a Boy Scout hatchet without a handle and a bald peen hammer.

We were working on a concrete surface which enabled the men to straighten the metal by hitting the corrugations with pieces of wood I had selected from the firewood to serve as hammers. After the material was partially flattened I used the hatchet and a hunk of wood to run a deep score 10 inches from the edge of the sheet. We then put wood under the edge of the sheet. Three of us went to the other end of the inclined sheet and walked up it until it bent at the score. I now had a piece of material 10 inches by about 40 inches. By scoring and bending I ended up with a blank 8″ x 10″. One of the men working with me was an almost blind BOR named Lem White. With the ball peen hammer, he enthusiastically and meticulously flattened the blank. I then rounded the corners of the rectangle so that, when the sides were bent up and the corners fluted, the top of the plate would be even all around. Lem White used the concrete floor to sand the blank. I whittled a form which enabled me to create the fluted corners. I was very pleased with the final product and so was Nigel Loring. He ordered 11 more and told me to give the 12 plates to Capt. Henderson, his adjutant, to distribute.

My crew worked rather leisurely, still we completed the job in three or four days and I gave the plates to Capt. Henderson. After a couple of days I asked Nigel if he wanted me to make any more. He said that Capt. Henderson didn't want me to make any more plates because I had given one to Lem White without his permission. I couldn't believe what I was hearing.

I said, "You have got to be kidding."

He replied, "No I'm not Jack."

I exploded, "That's the stupidest thing I've ever heard!"

Nigel said, "Did you think you Americans had a monopoly on stupid? Here is what I intend to do. I will appoint you the compound Pioneering Engineering Officer and you can occupy yourself in any way that is good for the compound. You will only answer to me. Is that all right?"

I said, "I don't know if I will be needed full-time. Let's see how it works out."

It turned out that I was very busy. The working parties expanded my tool chest by bringing in sheet metal shears and a hand saw. I found a way to make rivets out of the heavy copper wire that was available so I could do maintenance on the pots and pans that the kitchen used to cook and distribute our rice, jyp-oh and tea.

About noon each day, cans of food were delivered to our room so I made a practice of being there when it was being served. One day I was busy repairing a pot that was needed for cooking and I was probably a half an hour late getting to my room. I found my serving of food cold on the edge of my bed. I told myself not to use any profanity.

I then went to the center of the room and loudly announced, "Please give me your attention. I am the only officer in this room who is making the slightest attempt to improve the way of life for the prisoners in this compound. I don't want to ever again have to eat my food cold. If I am not here, wait for me. If you don't want to wait send someone out to find me because I'll be employed somewhere doing something to better conditions in this compound."

No one said a word, nonetheless, after my speech they never started serving the food unless I was present. I know some of the officers resented my attitude.

I was very surprised one day when Nigel Loring asked me if I would like to participate in a séance. I was surprised that I was being asked and even more surprised that Nigel would participate in such nonsense.

He explained to me that one of the Aussies had been a medium in Sydney and, with the spirits of all the deceased prisoners hanging around he might get one to participate. He said that four of us would meet in the kitchen after dark. I was so pleased to be invited that I told him I would be delighted to attend. I also had a great deal of curiosity about what happens at a séance.

That night we were seated around a heavy table on very rickety chairs. We placed our hands on the table so that my little finger on both hands touched the little fingers of Nigel on my right and someone on my left. I assume the medium was touching Nigel and the man on his right in the same way. I sat silently with my hands lightly touching the table as I had been told to do. After a considerable length of time the table tilted towards me.

The medium said, "A spirit wants to talk to you. If you ask questions he will answer with one knock for yes and two knocks for no."

The table went back level.

I asked if my mother was all right and the spirit knocked, "Yes."

I repeated the question about my father, brother and sister and the spirit answered, "Yes."

I asked if I would ever see my parents again and the answer was,"Yes."

I then asked if the war would be over in six months. There was no answer.

The medium said, "The spirit is gone."
The séance was over and we returned to our room. I found the experience very puzzling. I was very familiar with the

kitchen and I can't conceive of a way the medium could have tilted the table. I also wondered, if it was all a fake, what motivated the medium. I felt I was very lucky to have received positive answers to my questions. Whether they were meaningful or not, negative answers would probably have caused me to be depressed.

Although I had been in some iffy situations, I don't think I ever experienced fear until July 1944. A BOR was discovered in the latrine area vomiting and his bowels spewing liquid. He was diagnosed as having Asiatic cholera. When he was advised, the prison Commandant took action immediately:

No. 1 - All work parties were canceled.

No. 2 - Block #6 was quarantined and a very limited
        number of people were permitted in or out.

No. 3 - The sick BOR and a friend who volunteered
        were isolated in an empty building.

No. 4 - We were given acid to sanitize any area that
        had been soiled by the sick man.

The only two people in Block #6 who knew anything about cholera were Major Ramsey, because of his medical training and Nigel Loring who was a Major in the British Frontier Force and had been stationed in Burma for several years. I always believed that if you were better informed about something that frightens you your fears would be allayed. That didn't help when I learned that cholera was water borne and its symptoms appear in one to three days after being ingested. The victim suffers a horrible painful death in two or three days.

Nigel canceled the noonday meal. It was an excellent

way of getting everyone's complete attention. Everyone learned that the only protection was to only drink hot water and only eat hot food. He also designated an area outside the building where anyone who experienced a stomach disorder during the night would go and wait until morning to be diagnosed. The next morning two men were diagnosed with cholera and moved to the isolation building. There were no more cases diagnosed for a couple of days and during this time the Japanese vaccinated all the prisoners. Nigel told me he had never heard of such a vaccine but he certainly hoped it would be effective. The next morning the fourth case was diagnosed.

At midnight I experienced a slight stomach pain that grew into a stomach ache. I forced myself to do as I had been instructed. There was no one in the receiving area so I sat down about 10 yards away from the wall to see what was going to happen. After about 15 minutes Nigel Loring came and asked, "How long have you been here?"

I told him and he said we will have to wait an hour and if we didn't feel nauseous we could return to our room. I'm sure that was the longest hour I'll ever live.

Eventually Nigel asked me if I felt nauseous and, when I said I wasn't, he said,"Jack, if we had cholera we would be puking by now. Let's go back upstairs. "

The epidemic lasted about 10 days and 13 men died. I was not involved but the BOR's in Block #6 burned the bodies. When six days had elapsed without a new case the Commandant lifted the quarantine.

24 EQUALITY

A few days later Nigel came to my workshop and told me he had another problem with my senior officers. He said that one of them asked him to check because they believed that the British were getting more rice than the Americans. He said he would like me to see if the claim was valid.

I said, "Instead of putting up with this crap why don't you move some British into the American room and vicey - versey. That way any future conflict will be between room #1 and room #2 and not between Americans and British."

Nigel said for me to find some volunteers and he would do the same, even though he didn't have much hope of success. I knew immediately two men who would be delighted to move from room #2 to room #1. They were fighter pilots who, with their flight leader bailed out of the planes over enemy territory. This is their story.

The morning after their fighter group arrived in India, they were part of a four plane flight over enemy territory. The area over which they were flying has no landmarks so they were relying on dead reckoning. The leader of the flight, Major Lutz, got lost and, as fuel began to run low, one plane left the formation. The pilots of the three remaining planes ran out of fuel and were forced to ditch their planes. It was obvious the two men would rather be anywhere other than a room with Major Lutz. With an additional 3 or 4 volunteers the men were transferred to room #1 and officers from room #1 were moved to room #2. I got a new neighbor out of the deal, Lieut. Kenneth Spurlock. We quickly became very good friends. Ken was educated, bright, quick witted and could see the humorous side of almost everything. I must say that, prior to Ken's arrival, my only true friends among the officers were George Wilson and a P-38 pilot named Donald Humphrey. Nigel and I considered the move a tremendous success.

Ken was a survivor of a guerrilla campaign to disrupt Japanese supplies and communication. On February 8, 1942, 2000 men, mules and equipment under the command of General Orde Wingate launched a "deep penetration" into North Burma. Meticulous arrangements were made to resupply the troops by air , otherwise no provisions were made to evacuate sick or wounded soldiers. Gen. Wingate created six fighting columns of 300 men which operated independently of each other to harass the Japanese. Ken was the Officer in Charge of Signals in the Headquarters Brigade.

After six weeks, Gen. Wingate received orders to cease combat operations and return to India. He divided his Headquarters Brigade into dispersal groups of about 30 men and ordered them to separate from each other and find their way through the enemy lines back to India. For five days Wingate pushed his group to march long distances and some of his men, exhausted and with dysentery, dropped out. Ken was one of them.

After resting a day, Ken set out to find a friendly Burmese village. The area he was in was populated by Animist, as well as, Buddhist. He suddenly encountered three natives armed with crossbows. Ken knew that the Japanese had offered a reward for any of Wingate's men, dead or alive. When the natives aimed their weapons at him, Ken drew his revolver, aimed and fired. One of the natives fell and the others sought cover. Ken ran into the jungle and resumed his search for a friendly village. He eventually found one with a group of people sitting around a fire. He entered the village and, when he got close enough, realized that the people he saw were Japanese soldiers. Moments after he was captured one of the soldiers lunged at him with a rifle with a fixed bayonet. He dodged and the bayonet entered his armpit and came out of his shoulder. The wound was never treated until Ken reached Rangoon Prison. The only treatment available was to keep it clean. After months, it slowly healed.

While my crew continued making plates I found a way to make spoons which were as needed as the plates. I continued to repair containers that had been abandoned yet were sorely needed. In fact, I was so busy that I mentioned to Nigel that I needed help. He told me to choose anyone I wanted and they would be excused from work parties. I suggested Ken Spurlock.

Nigel said, "Jack, you can do better than that; but if you want him and he is agreeable, you've got him." Nigel was mistaken. Ken was hard working, skillful and a great partner.

By December 1944 the Japanese had moved their Zeros and the B-24's were making daylight raids at relatively low levels. On December 14th, a flight of B-29's raided Rangoon for the first time. There were 14 planes in echelon and the bombs of one plane collided when they were dropped. This caused a tremendous explosion that completely demolished four planes. It was heartbreaking to see the planes come down in flames and the parachutes opening all over the sky. About 14 survivors eventually were put into Block #5. There was a flurry of signaling between our compound and Block #5. The one thing we wanted to know was how much progress had been made by the British Army on the road to Rangoon. As I recall the only hard information I got from the signaling was that the latest popular song was "Don't Fence Me In".

The Pioneer Shop became quite proficient using our limited tools to make plates and spoons and jury rigged anvils to back the copper rivets. We started to laugh in disbelief however, when Major Ramsey asked us to make a "troche cannula". First of all, we didn't know what a "troche cannula" was and besides that, we couldn't make it.

Major Ramsey explained, "It is a medical device used to pierce body cavities. It consists of a small channel with a plunger through it. The plunger and channel together have a three cornered point. If I had one I could help the Beri-Beri patients by draining the water from their testicles. You see it does not have to be perfect, however it has to be small and extremely sharp so I can pierce the skin."

Ken and I agreed to try. A tin can was the only metal we could think of that would be thin enough to make the channel and I hadn't seen a tin can in the last two years. We told the work parties and in two or three days we had several cans.

Fabricating the channel, as we designed it, required a blank with dimensions far beyond our ability to calculate. We envisioned a small diameter wire with the metal wrapped around it. The metal would meet in a butt joint so the finished channel would have a crack the length of the tube which was 2 inches long. We cut several half-inch wide pieces of metal and practiced several ways to end up with a minimum space at the butt joint. After several attempts we succeeded in getting a tube through which a wire could slide rather tightly. Major Ramsey monitored our progress daily and insisted that we hurry. His impatience convinced us that he believed the device would help alleviate the pain and discomfort of some of his patients.

The only thing that remained to complete the device was to make a handle on one end and a very sharp point on the other. To create the point we tried all sorts of abrasives: the concrete where the plates were sanded, the brick wall between the compounds, the wall of the main building. Of course, it was slow and painstaking yet we succeeded in making a long sharp point that could easily puncture human skin and enter a body cavity. Dr. Ramsey used it and said it was as effective as any he'd used in private practice.

One day I was standing looking down the compound at a man doing the Madrasi squat and picking at the scabies on his ass.

Nigel walked up behind me and asked,"What are you Americans going to do about Fletcher Hart?"

I answered, "Probably bury him in a few months."

Nigel suggested, "Why don't you go talk to him because I think you will find he is worth saving."

To which I replied, "For Christ's sake, Nigel, everyone in this prison is worth saving if we had the supplies."

Nigel asked, "What supplies would you need?"

I told Nigel,"We would need soap, warm water and a proper application of Bluestone (copper sulfate)."

Nigel assured me that he would find some soap and give me some wood so I could warm some water. I explained to Fletcher what we proposed to do and put Sgt. Daley in charge of the project. Sgt. Daley's hands had healed and he had stretched the skin on them by exercising so that he could make a loose fist. Daley was not happy with this rather nasty job, but he agreed to do it. Fletcher was delighted with the attention he was receiving and warned me that we couldn't use Bluestone because it hurt too much. I explained to Fletcher that we were going to use a very weak solution of Bluestone and that it had to be applied whether or not it hurt.

Our supplies consisted of a piece of cloth about the size of a large handkerchief and a piece of soap twice the size of my thumb. A stumbling block occurred when Sgt. Hart would not allow Daley to apply the Bluestone solution, because he was not "hospital staff". I asked Master Sgt. Sidney Quick who was Major Ramsey's assistant to help me.

Sgt. Quick was, at 42 years, the oldest enlisted man flying combat in the Air Force. He had been a prominent attorney in Miami and was offered a commission of Colonel as a Judge Advocate of the Army. He had insisted on becoming a radio operator so he could fly combat. He agreed to apply the Bluestone to Sgt. Fletcher Hart.

We joked about the lack of entertainment in the compound and decided that watching Fletcher Hart protest and squirm would be fun.

Within two weeks the scabies were beginning to disappear.

25 CHRISTMAS '44

As I approached my third Christmas day in prison I knew it was going to be a gastronomic feast. Conditions continued to improve under the new Commandant. He allocated a steer to be divided between Block #3 and Block #6. We were fortunate because one of the RAF pilots from Australia had been a sheep rancher. He was a skilled butcher and, in addition to the meat, he retrieved the blood and intestines from the steer. He felt that the cooks would somehow or other make blood sausage. Our cooks were very resourceful. They planned to create a mixture that could be stuffed into the casings from the steer.

They requested from the Pioneer Shop a funnel that would help them make the sausages. I asked Ken to make whatever he thought they needed. Ken and I had been working together for several months and we had developed an unusual and staunch relationship. We disagreed and argued about everything from "When the war was going to end?" to "Einstein's Theory of Relativity." Our discussions were a lot of fun and made the time go by pleasantly.

When he showed me what he had made for the cooks. I said,"That is the ugliest thing I've ever seen. I would be embarrassed for anyone to know that was made in this shop. Give it to me."

Ken said defiantly,"This is what the cooks are going to use!"

I tried to take the funnel from him but he ran, with me chasing him, around the front of the building and down the other side. He stopped and much to the delight of the walking sick, we tussled. Ken and I were amongst the very few prisoners that could have engaged in such frivolous activity. We also were probably the only two silly enough to risk serious injury to have a little fun.

I had no doubt that the cooks would make a meal despite their limited resources that would, by our standing, be worthy of a Christmas celebration. They were an admirable group of men. Their routine each day required them to wake up two hours before Tenko and prepare the morning meal for 180 men. This might seem a little difficult under any circumstances. In that case it required entering a dark cold shed, building a fire, steaming the rice and preparing the jyp-oh and hot tea (water). The rice was invariably cooked properly except when, for short periods of time, they received rice contaminated with sweepings from the docks. While we did not receive a satisfying amount of rice in any of the three meals, the rice was consistently good. To prepare a meal the cooks used City water drawn from a spigot near the cook shed. I would drink water from this spigot but when it was not working I only drank the three cups of tea I was given daily.

To prepare each meal the cooks needed 30 gallons of clean water. Since bombs frequently disrupted the city water supply, the cooks were forced to carry the water from the central prison pumping station which was a considerable distance away from the cook shed. The cooks also managed the distribution of the food. A Mess Officer was assigned to see that everyone got a fair share of the food. Whenever I looked at the cooks I realized that they ate as much rice as they wanted and that their jyp-oh was a lot more nourishing than the jyp-oh I received. I believe they deserved the perk and possibly a medal or two for what they did.

Christmas 1944 turned out to be very successful. The food was different and good and we could have seconds and even thirds because the Japanese Commandant authorized the quartermaster to issue extra rations.

26 THE MARCH OUT

During the month of February 1945 the prison was suffering from a severe water shortage caused by the frequent air raids. It was common knowledge that the monsoons would start at the end of April or early May. I reasoned that with the proper gutters we could capture the runoff from a shed attached to the building. With Spurlock's help, I designed a system that would capture 20 feet of runoff and then convey it 15 feet over open ground to the water trough. The last 5 feet of the over ground gutter was detachable so that it would not be in place until the rainwater ran clear. It was the most ambitious project we ever undertook and very time-consuming. We knew that if we were successful we would have a continuing source for water.

On April 24 we completed the project and were waiting patiently for the monsoons to start. On April 25 at

12 noon we received orders from the Japanese to prepare to leave Rangoon by road at 4:00 PM. This order was a total surprise because we had no idea where the Allied forces were located. The Japanese opened their stores and we had access to a large supply of used clothing and poorly made canvas shoes. I still had my Army uniform which, while some the worst from wear, was far better than what was available from the Japanese. I also had the beautiful boots I had received from Jock Ferrier.

I wasn't concerned or involved in organizing the prisoners for the march. The Japanese instructed Nigel to prepare a list of men who were capable of marching because the lame would be left behind. I was concerned about George Wilson because, although he had lost a lot of weight, he was still reasonably fit. I asked George which he would rather do: walk or stay. George asked me if he had a choice. I told him that Nigel Loring had treated me as if I was the commanding officer of the Americans and seemed to respect my opinion. George decided he would be better off if he was classified as lame. I found Nigel Loring and he accepted my opinion that George should stay in Rangoon. He also told me that Spurlock and I would be in charge of the enlisted personnel from Block #6.

Sometime later Sgt. Hart approached me and said,"When I am killed I want you to know you are responsible."

I said, "What the hell are you talking about?"

"I've been classified," he said "as fit to march and I wouldn't be if I still had my scabies and jungle sores!"

I told him I would see what I could do. I approached Nigel and asked if he could drop Fletcher from the fit list and he did.

When we organized the formation at 4 PM (1600 hours) 400 prisoners were divided into squadrons, platoons, companies or what have you. In the front were the hand-drawn carts that carried, in addition to the Japanese gear, food and cooking equipment. After the carts were the cooks and a group of prisoners who were to take turns pulling the carts. After them were Brig. Hobson and the officers from Block #3. The next group was Nigel Loring in charge of the officers from Block #6. The next group was the Allied enlisted personnel from Block #6, me and Spurlock were in charge of this group. Somewhere behind us were the survivors of the B-29 disaster and new arrivals that had been confined to solitary confinement.

The formation, after sitting in place for two hours, started to march at a very reasonable pace. We marched about an hour and during that time I knew I had made a serious mistake wearing my beautiful boots. When we stopped Ken took my left boot between his legs and I pushed on his fanny. After a couple of tries the boot came off. He took the other boot between his legs and I pushed, still we couldn't get the boot off my foot. Our rest period was over so I began walking with one bare foot and one booted foot. I was very concerned because obviously I couldn't march for days with 1 foot in the boot. I told Ken that when we next stopped if he would get enough prisoners around me, I could use my knife to cut the leather and remove the boot. At the next stop, in a coordinated move, I was surrounded and sat down to cut the leather. I found out that my foot was encased in steel reinforcements which were covered with leather. I remember I panicked. I felt I had just been given a death sentence. Although I can't remember the details, Ken removed the boot. When I looked at my foot I could see that my toenails were floating on blisters. I walked barefoot for the next 60 miles, I remember being grateful that the soles of my feet were very tough after being barefoot for over 2 1/2 years.

At about two o'clock in the morning we reached our bivouac area and remained there until 6 PM on the 26th of April. During the day cooks prepared food and tea for us and the Japanese. This was the timetable for the 27th and 28th except that we had no food or drink after we reached the bivouac area on the 28th.

I was told that there were 380 prisoners being moved and no one knew our proposed destination. We knew that the Japanese were retreating, still we had no idea where the Allied troops were in relation to Rangoon. For me the march was divided into the daylight, when we rested, and darkness, when we marched.

Two or three times each night British Hurricanes would fly over the road seeking targets We could hear them as they approached and would leave the road and lie face down on the ground to avoid being seen. Absent the activity and anxiety caused by the planes the nights were long, arduous and monotonous. This was no walk in the park with beautiful scenery on either side. The only thing we occasionally saw was a burned out vehicle. I don't know if there is a proper word to describe what I experienced as I walked. I didn't do anything consciously, yet I went into some sort of trance or self-hypnotism where my mind was not connected to the pain I experienced. I marched on unaware of the elapsed time and only a mild awareness of the discomfort in my body and feet.

Since we arrived at the bivouacs in the dark, daylight brought with it a lot of activity. The cooks were amazingly efficient and we received much-needed food and water. The Japanese guards were posted around the area so that there was not a great deal, if any, co-mingling. There were reports, or more precisely, rumors that men had dropped out and were never heard of again. Most of the white prisoners were ahead of me in the line and I don't remember passing any that had dropped out during the nights. I am absolutely certain that if men fell the guards would have to choose whether or not to leave them alive. Through Nigel Loring I was given information that Brig. Hobson, Col. Powell and several other senior officers had planned for us to make a mass escape after we crossed the river at Pegu. They had decided that the Japanese intended to move us to Thailand and if we escaped and went North we would encounter friendly Karenna natives.

While we were marching the night of the 27th I received 10 ounces of water. I was disappointed to learn from the cooks that we were not to receive any food or water until we reached the bivouac.

There was a good deal of low-flying aircraft over our bivouac. I spent the morning resting, trying not to be hungry and thirsty, which is rather difficult to do. About three o'clock Nigel Loring woke me up to brief me. He said that a patrol, sent by the commandant, reported we were 3 miles from Pegu and, despite the fact that the city was bombed and deserted, the bridge was intact. He also advised me that the plans to escape remained the same. He then informed me that the supply carts would be dropped and we wouldn't have any food or water until the 29th. Since I had been without water for over 24 hours, this was very distressing. I realized as I had so many times before that as a POW I had to accept adversity and try to ameliorate the consequences. When we left Rangoon I had made a sling to carry my mess kit. To make a positive response to the discouraging information I decided to lighten my load by discarding the sling. This left me with the clothes I was wearing, my pocket knife and my homemade pipe. I slept a great deal during the day, however, I was aware that I hadn't seen Ken Spurlock since we reached the bivouac.

27 RESCUED

At twilight the guards called for Tenko. When we lined up in three squads of 20 men (10 front, 10 back) I was immediately aware that we were short 10 men and Ken Spurlock. I announced very loudly that we were short 10 men and to keep moving around so I couldn't get an accurate count. After a very confused roll call during which the guard was shouting and I was probably trembling, Nigel Loring arrived. He said to me that 18 men were missing from the work party group and for me to do a proper roll call and report the number to him. I did as I was told and he gave the number to the guard. He then asked me if I wanted him to send an officer to replace Ken. I told him it was not necessary and asked Sgt. Higginbotham to replace Ken.

It took about an hour of marching to reach the bridge at Pegu. Sgt. Higginbotham, a B-24 crew chief and I talked constantly exchanging information about families and our lives before joining the service. He was aware of the plans to escape and we agreed to stay together when we were freed.

As we crossed the bridge at Pegu we saw that Japanese soldiers were preparing to blow up the bridge. About five minutes later we heard the explosion that destroyed the bridge. The road we were walking on was adjacent to the railroad tracks. The guards walked on the tracks which were 6 feet above the road. I recognized that this was a situation where the guards with machine guns could massacre us. I was not concerned because I was convinced they intended to keep us alive and prisoners.

When we entered a deserted village six hours later we were tired, hungry and terribly thirsty. The guards had joined us and we were still in our formations. The commandant called for the group leaders to assemble. He then dismissed everyone except Brig. Hobson and Nigel Loring. A short time later he, his interpreter, and the rest of the guards walked away. Moments later Brig. Hobson announced we were free.

It was a moment of euphoria and no one felt tired, hungry or thirsty. We still had three or four hours before daylight. We had no idea where we were in relation to the British advance from Mandalay to Rangoon. I was told that the senior British officers thought we were near populated villages and in the morning the Burmese would contact us and provide food and water.

At dawn a full-scale battle erupted about 5 miles east of our village. We heard all the sounds of battle; planes, bombs, cannons, machine guns and rifle fire. Someone had given me some tobacco and I was smoking a pipe when Nigel Loring approached me, "Jack, some RAF officers are putting up some signs that will alert Allied pilots that we are here."

I said, "In my opinion nothing would be as effective as POW or SOS! "

No sooner had I made the statement when we heard bombs explode and machine gun fire. We jumped behind a tree and when the planes passed over I ran out of the back of the village towards another village about a half a mile away. I ran about 300 yards and was passing the lone tree between the villages when I heard the machine gun fire. I threw myself behind the tree and said a Catholic prayer,"Jesus, Mary and Joseph save me now!"

I saw where the bullets were striking the ground and I chastised myself, "You know better than that!" Bullets struck about 6 feet in front of the tree on both sides and about seven or 8 feet past the tree. I got up and ran like hell and reached the next village.

I was in a shed of some kind when BOR's began to arrive. Eventually there were 11 BOR's, Sgt. Ben Lucas, an American, and me. It occurred to me that I really was the luckiest person in the world or the unluckiest depending on how you look at being responsible for the welfare of others.

I was the only officer with 12 enlisted personnel who wanted to know from me, "What do we do now, Mr. Horner?"

I told them that if the village was occupied someone would contact us in a few minutes and I would negotiate for some food and water. I was surprised to see that some of them were still carrying their mess kits. The Burmese elder that approached me spoke English. I asked him if he could advise the British that ex-prisoners of war were in his village and the one we left.

He insisted that there was no way that he could help me contact the British. I then negotiated for food and drink. He drove a hard bargain, to which I agreed, because we needed the rations badly. For 100 rupees ($30) per man he would supply unlimited food and water and a Japanese rifle which we could use for our protection. I signed a note and after a while we had plenty to eat and drink and a rifle without ammunition. I tried to get a consensus from my troops as to whether we stay where we are or return to the village we left. Sgt. Ben Lucas said he thought we should stay because there was no assurance that there was food or water if we returned to the first village. I agreed and instructed them to follow me into the village and make themselves comfortable. If Japanese soldiers entered the village they were to simply meld with the natives. In the early afternoon two Burmese approached and as they got close I recognized the senior American officer, Major Lutz, in Burmese clothing. He said he was convinced that the Burmese accompanying him would help him contact the British troops. I asked if I could help him in any way and he said he had everything under control.

All afternoon I wondered whether the decision to stay in the village was a good one. I finally decided that the die had been cast and I would get some much-needed sleep. The sun was setting when the head man approached me. He was very excited and concerned. He said, "There are British tanks lined up outside the village and they are getting ready to fire cannons at us. You must go out and tell them that there are no Japanese here!"

I went to the edge of the village and saw that there were eight vehicles in a line about 200 yards from the village. I knew that they had to be British because the Japanese were retreating and would never act offensively against a peaceful village. I told the head man to get me a flag of truce. He quickly handed me a white cloth tied to a short bamboo pole.

Suddenly, Sgt. Lucas said, "If you order me, I'll go out to the vehicles." I knew I should go but my bare feet hurt.

I said, "Okay Sgt. Lucas, I order you to go and explain our situation."

By now we could barely see the vehicles. Sgt. Lucas walked away through waist high grass and eventually we could no longer see him. A short time later he came back to where I was standing and said that the officer he met wanted to see me.

When I got close enough I held out my hand and said, "I'm Lieut. Kenneth Horner of the United States Air Force."

He said, "I'm Capt. Bell of the Gurkha Rifles."

I said, "Are you by any chance nicknamed Dinga?"

He said, "All British officers named Bell are nicknamed Dinga."

I said, "I asked because I was in prison with a British officer who often talked about a Dinga Bell. His name is Ken Spurlock."

He said, "My God! Is Spurlock still alive?"

I replied, "He was the last time I saw him."

Capt. Bell then said, "This is what we'll do Lieutenant.

You get as many men together as you can and send them to me in a single line with no guns or weapons of any kind."

I explained that the prisoners were disbursed over a large area and it might take some time to gather them. He assured me they would wait and to take my time.

When I got back to the village I immediately sent two BOR's to the original village to see if they could find Major Loring or Brig. Hobson to advise them of the rescue operation. While we waited I explained to the head man that I had prevented the British from shelling the village and I wanted him to return the note I had given him for food and water. He said he tore up the note when I sent Sgt. Lucas to the vehicles.

The 2 BOR's that I had sent returned and reported that they had found Maj. Loring and many of the POWs and Maj. Loring wanted to see me before he moved them.

I said to myself "SHIT!" and moving as fast as I could I found Nigel Loring. He immediately asked, "Are you sure Jack?"

I said , "Hell YES! Nigel, a Capt. Bell is in charge. He wants me to send the men out to the trucks in a single line with no guns or weapons."

Nigel ordered everyone to follow us in a formation of four men abreast. As we walked I mentioned that I hadn't seen Brig. Hobson. Nigel said that he was hit and killed instantly during the morning air raid.

I said, "That's tough luck after 3 1/2 years of being a prisoner. Was anyone else killed?"

Nigel replied, "It's almost unbelievable, but no one

else was killed or wounded."

When we reached the edge of the village I asked Nigel to keep his troops in formation until I dispatched the men that were with me. I told them Sgt. Lucas would go first and they would follow him in a single line. Nigel instructed his group to follow. When Marshall Foster's turn came he stepped out of line and asked if he could wait for me. Nigel said okay and when the last man went by, Nigel, Marshall and I followed him.

The trucks moved about 7 or 8 miles before we were unloaded. We were immediately given cigarettes, chocolate candy, K-Rations and soft drinks. I was very careful not to over indulge. Marshall talked to one of the Gurkhas in Urdu and was told that we should sleep under one of the trucks.

As I went to sleep I heard the chattering of a nearby machine gun, yet I felt perfectly safe.

28 FREEDOM

Ihad been living in an uninformed cloistered environment for almost 3 years so the speed with which things happened was absolutely amazing to me. In early morning on the 30th, I boarded a United States Air Force plane and by mid-morning I had a shave, bath, and haircut. At noon, as I sat on my bed eating a steak and potatoes lunch, I learned that George and the rest of the POW's had been rescued. By early afternoon I was issued underwear, khaki uniform and shoes. By mid afternoon a finance officer gave me a wallet and $250 of my pay.

I remember taking a long nap and when I woke up I chatted with a nurse whose hometown was New Orleans. I mentioned to her that my life would be complete if I had a gin and tonic or a rum and coke. She informed me that there was an Officers Mess where I could get drinks after dinner. She also informed me that I could send a very short telegram to my parents. After supper, Don and I went to the mess and thoroughly enjoyed ourselves drinking and dancing with the nurses. It was a very interesting and satisfying day!

On the morning of May 1st I had a slight headache (hangover) so I didn't dress until I was told by the nurses that General Stratemeyer was coming to give Smith Radcliffe and me the Silver Star. After I received the award Don Humphrey, myself and a couple of other prisoners were given permission to visit Killarny Estates, an Army Rest and Recreation facility in Calcutta.

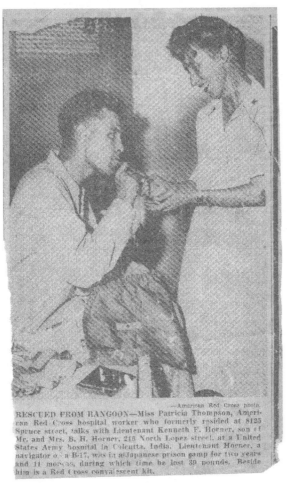

—American Red Cross photo.
RESCUED FROM RANGOON—Miss Patricia Thompson, American Red Cross hospital worker who formerly resided at 8125 Spruce street, talks with Lieutenant Kenneth F. Horner, son of Mr. and Mrs. B. H. Horner, 218 North Lopez street, at a United States Army hospital in Calcutta, India. Lieutenant Horner, a navigator on a B-17, was in a Japanese prison camp for two years and 11 months, during which time he lost 30 pounds. Beside him is a Red Cross convalescent kit.

Dateline May 1, 1945, New Orleans Louisiana.

In mid- afternoon my Father reads a telegram he has received.

He shouts ,"Jeanne, Jeanne, JEANNE! They found him, they found Kenneth!"

Both cry as they rush into each other's arms and hold each other tight. After a while my mother says ,"Harry, I must go to our room and thank God"

She goes to their bedroom and my Father sits in his chair feeling relaxed and happy for the first time in years.

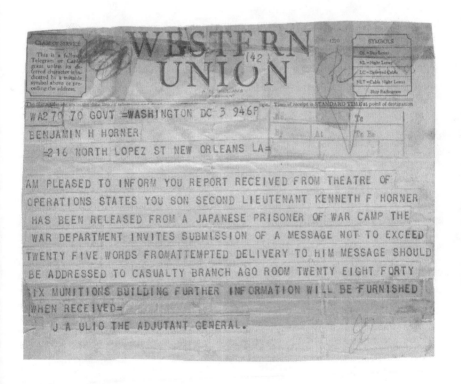

Nearly an hour passes and he receives another telegram. He goes to where my mother is praying and kneels beside her .

He whispers, "Thank God some more because I just received a telegram from Kenneth saying that he is well and fit."

My mother nods and continues to pray.

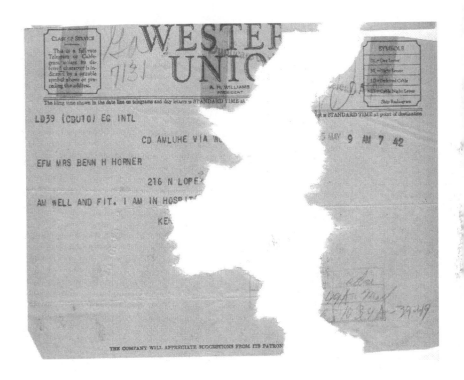

EPILOGUE
and
LAGNIAPPE

EPILOGUE

A few days ago I finished writing MIA. A task I undertook because of the repeated requests of my wife and daughter. To avoid the additional work of editing, I sent copies of the document to four friends. They did an excellent job and found fault because I didn't complete the story.

As a matter of fact I did not know the fate of the prisoners that stayed in Rangoon until May 1, the same day my parents were notified that I was alive.

On April 26, the day after the "healthy" prisoners departed, the remaining prisoners discovered that there were no Japanese guards. They found a note left by the Japanese that said they were free, had permission to use all the Japanese supplies, and hoped they would meet again on the field of battle.

They painted signs on two of the buildings. The sign on one building said "JAPS GONE". The sign on another building said "EXTRACT DIGIT" which translated from British to American meant "TAKE YOUR FINGER OUT!'

They were rescued the next day by Gurkha troops and loaded on a British vessel to be transported to Calcutta. On May 6, 1945, while I was in the hospital in Calcutta, Germany surrendered.

On August 6, 1945, while I was on leave in New Orleans an atomic bomb was dropped on the Japanese city of Hiroshima. A few days later another bomb was dropped on Nagasaki and the Japanese surrendered unconditionally.

George Wilson and I never saw each other again, however we kept in touch by letters and phone. He never regained the hearing in his right ear. After several years, he left the service and became president of an insurance business owned by his family. He married and had three children.

John Boyd weighed only 99 pounds when he left Rangoon prison. He recovered and stayed in the service until he retired as a Master Sergeant. He then started a very successful real estate business in Mayfield, Kentucky. He served two terms as Mayor. He married and had children. We stayed in touch and met several times.

Private Smith Radcliff remained in the service and was stationed at MacDill Field in Tampa, Florida. We saw each other frequently because he spent his weekends partying at my apartment. Smitty eventually married a Tampa girl and had two daughters. He received orders and moved to Las Vegas. He retired as a Master Sergeant.

Capt. Marshall Foster and I parted on the morning of April 30 promising to keep in touch. That is about all we did until sometime in the 1960s. He had married and had a daughter. He had become the president of a shipping company that carried containers from New York to Liverpool. His offices were in New York. I received a letter addressed To the Occupant, 36 Spanish Main, Tampa, Florida. The letter was from Barbara Foster, Marshall's wife. It said "I have been trying to reach a man named Kenneth Horner who was married and had four children and lived at this address prior to you. I hope you can advise me where he can be reached. Please call me collect at 525 - 6806." Apparently some mail had gone astray. In any case, I immediately contacted Marshall and we visited him in New York. We then communicated regularly and he visited me in Tampa and my wife and I visited him in Aldershot, England.

Harold Goad returned to Kansas City to discover that his wife, Helen, had married his best friend a year after he was declared dead. A Judge ruled that Helen was legally married to both men and that she could choose which man she wanted and he would annul one of the marriages. Helen chose Harold. They moved to Miami where he became a pilot for Eastern Air Lines.

Master Sergeant Fletcher Hart left the Army and became a radio operator for Eastern Airlines in Miami.

Betty showed up! I had been in New Orleans for two or three weeks when one day, at 3 PM, I received a phone call from my fiancée, Betty. She said she was at the St. Charles Hotel, room 352, and that she would love to see me. Because my only means of transportation was the Canal Street streetcar, I had about an hour to consider our engagement. I decided I had no choice but to wait and see. When Betty opened the door she looked absolutely stunning. We exchanged civilities and then Betty said, "Aren't you going to kiss me."

We kissed and she said, "I know you are wondering why I'm here Jack and I want you to know it's to return the engagement ring you gave me. You will recall that I met Capt. Sharp in Tampa and from reading countless descriptions of his flight, I knew you were missing in action.

Anyway, I started dating and I got married and divorced. I then started dating again, got married and divorced a second time."

Betty had been speaking slowly and in a somber manner. She suddenly appeared to switch gears.

Laughingly she said, "So you see Jack, I'm really not ready to try a third time. There is Brandy on the night table and I suggest we have a drink to our disengagement."

After the drink there was no serious conversation. We laughed, joked, went out to dinner and I spent the night. In the morning, she ordered breakfast from room service.

Rather suddenly she announced, "Jack I have to catch the shuttle and I want to say goodbye here."

I responded, "Goodbye" or "Au Revoir!"

She stood up and took a couple of steps towards the door. She turned and answered , "We are not going to meet again, Jack, this is goodbye."

I stood up and she kissed me lightly on my lips and

pushed me away but still had her outstretched hands on my shoulders. She made me promise to have another cup of coffee before I left the room. She turned and walked out of the door and my life forever. I turned to get the cup of coffee and saw she had left the engagement ring on the table. I sat down puzzled by the purpose of her visit. If it was to return the ring and end our engagement, she could have accomplished that with a "Dear John Letter" and enclosed the ring. I believe she concocted the marriage nonsense so that she could orchestrate our meeting to give her a feeling of closure. I believe she was married and probably had children. After all, three years is a long time.

She gave me my freedom, yet I didn't feel tremendously happy. Instead of coffee I made myself a Café Royale. As I slowly consumed my drink, I realized that my rescue put her in a position somewhat similar to the one experienced by Helen Goad. She had a husband she loved and a superfluous fiancé that she also loved. I made myself another drink.

Don Humphrey lived in St. Louis Missouri so we saw each other frequently. We fished together dozens of times. He became president of the largest brick manufacturer and distributor in the Midwest. He married and had three daughters. We ended a tour of France that we enjoyed with our wives in Cardiff, Wales as guests of the Spurlock's.

Nigel Loring and I never saw each other again after we reached Allied control on the night of the 29th of April. For a short while I swapped letters with some BOR's that I knew and one of them said that Nigel Loring had been diagnosed with some strange disease that required a strict regimen of diet and medication. He treated his illness with wine, women and song. He didn't live a full year after we were recovered.

Weno was tried and found guilty of brutal war crimes. I made a deposition regarding his brutality and learned later that he was indeed punished by hanging.

Ken Spurlock was missing when we did Tenko at dusk on the 28th of April along with 10 BOR's. I later learned that Ken and five or six BOR's were in the jungle for seven days before being led back to the Pegu Road by friendly villagers. Ken went back to school and graduated as an electrical engineer. He joined the British Telephone and Postal Department. In 1960 he was given a sabbatical so that he could serve as Managing Director of the Jamaican Telephone Company. With my wife and two youngest children, I visited him, his wife and two daughters in Kingston. He returned to Britain and became Chairman of the Wales Telephone Company. Over the years we have met at least a dozen times in Europe and the United States. On several occasions Don Humphrey joined us.

Amazingly, Ken and I have seen and talked to each other recently using a fantastic electronic software program called Skype.

Sydney Quick returned to Miami. He had been declared dead and the insurance paid to his sister. He had to reimburse the government for $10,000 she'd received. After I moved to Tampa he gave me a key so that I could use his apartment when I was in Miami. We enjoyed visiting bars and nightclubs together and having a few drinks until his fiancée cautioned me "Jack, you know you have a perfect right to be intoxicated in public and raise hell in any way you choose, but Sydney is a very prominent attorney and that kind of behavior is not going to help his career.

I said "Alright, Rose, we will drink and solve the world's problems at home."

We stayed in touch and visited each other until he died.

As for me, in late 1945 I was ordered to Miami Beach to be either discharged or reassigned. I chose to leave the service and was given a discharge that was to be effective after three months. During that time I was invited to join four men from New Orleans who were forming a corporation to manufacture aluminum jalousies.

Two of the four were to be absentee stock holders. As strange as it seems, they did not trust each other and, as a result, I was elected President. A year later, with the help of Sydney Quick I sold my stock. I moved to Tampa Florida and started a new company that manufactured jalousies and windows.

The company, Nu-Air Manufacturing, lasted 62 years until it was closed in 2008 due to the slowdown in house building in Florida. I married a wonderful woman, divorced after the war, who had three children, two boys and a girl. We were blessed with a fourth child, a girl, born on April 25, 1955, exactly 10 years to the day that I marched out of Rangoon Prison.

With my wife, Conchita Vega Horner

LAGNIAPPE
(a little extra!)

Since my memoir is rather short I have added copies of a few of the original Army transcripts which may be of interest to the reader. It was a year from the time that I enlisted as a Flying Cadet that I was commissioned as a 2nd Lieutenant. The extract shown at right both commissioned me and ordered me to active duty as an officer.

The monthly pay for a second Lieut. was $160 and I immediately made an allotment to my parents of $100. I did not receive any pay prior to being shot down as the following "Pay and Allowance Account" shows. (page 166)

The Report of Physical Examination was done on May 17th, 18 days after I became a patient at the 142nd General Hospital in Calcutta. My first day at the hospital I weighed 128 lbs. According to the records I gained 17 pounds in 19 days. The day I became a prisoner I weighed 155 lbs.(pages 168-169)

The extract awarding me the Silver Star is dated July 15, 1942. The picture shows Smith Radcliff and me receiving it three years later in the hospital. (Pages 170-171)

67 years have passed and I can't believe or explain why I wrote this letter. I suspect I felt that I had not done enough as a soldier. The OSS approved the transfer but the Commanding Officer did not. (Pages 172-173)

Ten months after I executed a note to Maung Tun Myaing he tried to collect it. He had agreed on the night of April 19, 1945 in his village to destroy the note if I contacted the British. I explained the circumstances surrounding the note to the fiscal officer in India-Burma. The claim was denied. (Page 175)

Following is a newspaper article, a picture of my parents and a collage of newspaper articles regarding my being found, photographs of the prison and some of the inmates and finally a cartoon depiction of the air battle over Rangoon. (176-181)

AIR BASE HEADQUARTERS MACDILL FIELD
Office of the Base Commander

                                                    Tampa, Florida,
                                                    January 7, 1942,

NUMBER   7)

E X T R A C T

X   X   X

14. Confirming the verbal order of the Commanding Officer, January 5, 1942.
By direction of the President, each of the following named Second Lieutenants, Air
Corps Reserve, now at MacDill Field, Tampa, Florida, are ordered to active duty
effective January 5, 1942. On that date each officer will report to the Commanding
Officer, MacDill Field, Tampa, Florida, for assignment to duty. Each officer will
rank from January 5, 1942.

                    *   *   *
               2nd Lt. KENNETH FOSTER HORNER, (ASN Unknown)
               216 North Lopez Street, New Orleans, La.

                    *   *   *

        The above named Second Lieutenants are assigned to the 9th Bombardment
Squadron, Sierra Bombardment Group and will report for duty accordingly.

X   X   X

                    By order of Colonel YOUNG:

                                            W.J. McCOMB,
                                            Captain, Air Corps,
                                            Assistant Adjutant.

OFFICIAL:
        s/ W. J. McCOMB,
        Captain, Air Corps,
        Assistant Adjutant

D. O. Vou. No. _____

PAID BY
J. M. ROGERS, JR
1st Lt., F. D.
Rec. Sta. No. 6
Camp Shelby, Miss.
SEP 1945

WAR DEPARTMENT
Form No. 336b—Revised
Form approved by Comptroller General, U. S.
September 25, 19__

WAR DEPARTMENT

PAY AND ALLOWANCE ACCOUNT

(Commissioned Officers, Army Nurses, Warrant Officers, Contract Surgeons)

APPROPRIATIONS:
212/60425   XXXXXXXXXXXXX 601-60 P 411-01 599-999 P 5593.34
Fried to 1st 26 / 61 28f 14, per ltr, OO AAF, Washington, DO
atd 5 Jun/45

(1) THE UNITED STATES, Pr, 1st Lt AC ORC Recepn Sta 5 O-435393

Sta. No. 4394

To: _____
(Rank and organization)

(2) Station Cp Shelby, Miss   Station No. 1979 AAF BU

On duty at present station per Par 24 Jun/45, S. O. No. 173, Hdqrs. Ft Totten, NY 24 June, 19 45
Departed from Ft Totten, NY 24 Jun, 19__. Reported for duty at Cp Shelby, Miss 26 June, 19 45

DEPENDENTS: NONE
(3) Lawful wife _____ or
(State her Christian or given name in full and husband's surname and her address each month.)
Unmarried children under 21 years of age _____

(State names, ages, and addresses each month. Evidence of dependency attached hereto or filed with voucher No. _____,
19____, accounts of _____)
(4) Dependent mother _____
(State her Christian or given name in full and husband's surname and her address each month)
During the current period for which allowances are claimed on account of my dependent mother I have contributed to her
support the sum of $_____, in cash or its equivalent, without any consideration in return, which contribution
is her chief support, and each and every statement set forth in her affidavit dated _____, 19____
(attached hereto), filed with voucher for the month of _____, 19____, is true and correct, and so
remains at this time, except _____
(State fully changes occurring between date of last affidavit and signing of this voucher)

(5) For over 9 years' service; _____ pay period; _____ years completed on _____, 19__.

CREDITS:				AMOUNT
(6) For base and longevity pay from Active Service 1 March 42 to 30 June 45				$ 6152 92
(7) For additional pay for Flying Pay from 1 March, 19 42, to 24 June, 19 45	from 29 March, 19 42, to 20 April, 19 45			587 22
				3173 74
(8) For pay for _____ mount, _____ from _____, 19__, to _____, 19__.				
of which I was the actual and exclusive owner, which (was or were) suitable for the military service, and maintained at _____				
(9) For subsistence allowance from 1 March, 19 42, to 30 June, 19 45				843 42
(10) For rental allowance from _____, 19__, to _____, 19__.				

during which period I was not assigned adequate quarters at my permanent station; if without dependents,
I was not on field or sea duty; if with dependents, I did not occupy with them any public quarters assigned
to me without charge at any station, nor did any of them occupy public quarters assigned to them or to any
other officer or his dependents, except for bona fide social visits.

TOTAL CREDITS ... $ 10757 34

DEBITS:		AMOUNT
(11) Class "D" Government Insurance Premium for Feb/42 to Jun/45 See Reverse.	$ 4100 00	
(12) Class "E" Allotment $5.00 mo fr Mar/42 to Jun/42	64 00	
(13) Class "N" National Service Life Insurance See Reverse	500 00	
(14) Due United States for _____		

TOTAL DEBITS ... 5164 00

NET BALANCE ... $ 5593 34

(15) On _____ (ordinary or sick) leave or absence; Departed _____, 19__, under Par. _____, S. O. No. _____,
Hdqrs. _____, 19____; extended by Par. _____, S. O. No. _____, Hdqrs. _____
_____, 19____; Returned _____, 19__

(16) I certify that the foregoing statement and account are true and correct; that payment therefor has not been received; and that
payment to me as stated on the within pay voucher is not prohibited by any provisions of law limiting the availability of the
appropriation(s) involved.

811 St Louis St.
New Orleans, La.
Date _____, 19__
(SIGN ORIGINAL ONLY)   MEMORANDUM Lt AC

(17) I certify that during the period for which rental allowance is claimed on this voucher the above officer was not assigned adequate
quarters at his permanent station.

Date _____, 19__
(SIGN ORIGINAL ONLY, ON MEMORANDUM, TYPE OR PRINT NAME AND RANK)
Name _____
Rank _____
Commanding Officer

(18) Paid by { Check(s) No.(s) 1136VVOV, dated 17 SEP, 19 5, for $ 5593.34, on Treasurer of the United States in favor of payee named above.
{ Cash, $_____, on _____, 19__
(SIGN ORIGINAL ONLY)
10-15821

MEMORANDUM

THE
PRESIDENT
OF
THE UNITED STATES OF AMERICA

To all who shall see these presents, greeting:

Know Ye, that reposing special trust and confidence in the patriotism, valor, fidelity and abilities of _____Kenneth Foster Horner_____,

I do appoint him _____Second Lieutenant, Air Corps_____ in the

Army of the United States

such appointment to date from the _____fifth_____ day of _____January_____ nineteen hundred and _____forty-two_____. He is therefore carefully and diligently to discharge the duty of the office to which he is appointed, by doing and performing all manner of things thereunto belonging.

He will enter upon active duty under this commission only when specifically ordered to such active duty by competent authority.

And I do strictly charge and require all Officers and Soldiers under his command when he shall be employed on active duty, to be obedient to his orders as an officer of his grade and position. And he is to observe and follow such orders and directions, from time to time, as he shall receive from me, or the future President of the United States of America, or the General or other Superior Officers set over him, according to the rules and discipline of War.

This commission evidences an appointment in the Army of the United States, under the provisions of section 37, National Defense Act, as amended, and is to continue in force for a period of five years from the date above specified, and during the pleasure of the President of the United States, for the time being.

Done at the City of Washington, this _____fifth_____ day of _____January_____ in the year of our Lord one thousand nine hundred and _____forty-two_____, and of the Independence of the United States of America the one hundred and _____sixty-sixth_____.

By the President:

J. H. Powell

Adjutant General.

REPORT OF PHYSICAL EXAMINATION
(See AR 40-100 and 40-105)

Instructions :—Unless otherwise prescribed, this form will be used for all physical examinations of officers, nurses, or warrant officers ; applicants for appointment as such in the Regular Army, National Guard, or Officers' Reserve Corps; and enrollment in the Reserve Officers Training Corps. Use typewriter if practicable. Attach plain additional sheets if required.

1. **Horner, Kenneth F.** **O-435,393**
   (Last name)   (First name)   (Middle name)   (Serial number)

2. **2D Lt** .... **88th Rec Sq,7th Bomb Gp** Age.... **26** ....Years of service.... **4** ....
   (Grade)   (Organization and arm or service)   (Nearest birthday)   (Whole number only)

3. Name of examination¹.... **Special** ....Component of Army²... **ORC**

4. Typhoid vaccination. No. series completed.... **2** ....Last series.... **7 May** ...., 19. **45**

5. Date of last smallpox vaccination.. **4 May 1945** ....Type of reaction.... **Immune**

6. Other vaccination or immunity tests..**Cholera, Tetanus, Typhus, Yellow fever**

7. Medical history³.....**Childhood diseases: Unidentified convulsions (1925 ?)**
   Serious Illnesses : None
   Operations: Broken nose repair (1938); Tonsillectomy (1930)
   Injuries: Broken nose
   Family History: Negative

8. Eyes..... **Normal**
   Distant vision : Right 20/.**15**....correctible to 20/ ....by....
   (Snellen type) Left 20/.**15** ....correctible to 20/ ....by....
   Near vision : Right J-//-...**I** ....correctible to 1-//-........by....
   (Jaeger type) Left J-//-...**I** ....correctible to 1-//-........by....
   Refraction⁵ (under cycloplegia) : Right... **Not indicated** ....Left....
   Color perception (red and green)...... **Normal**

9. Ears ..... **Normal**
   Hearing (low coversational voice) : Right **15/15** Left **15/15** Audiometer (percent loss) : Right...... Left...

10. Nose and Throat.. **Normal**

11. Teeth :⁷   Right   (Examinee's)   Left
    X 7 6 5 4 3 2 1 1 2 3 4 5 6 (7) 8
    XX XX XX 13 12 11 10 9 9 10 11 XX 13 XX(15)XX
    Remarks, including other defects...... **None**
    Indicate : Restorable carious teeth by 0 ; nonrestorable carious teeth by / ; missing natural teeth by x.
    ....Classification.... **II**

    Prosthetic dental appliances...... **None**

12. Posture .... **Good** ....Figure....... **Medium** ....Frame.... **Medium**
    (Excellent, good, fair, bad.)   (Slender, medium, stocky, obese)   (Light, medium, heavy)

13. Temperature **98.4** ..Height **68-3/4** inches. Weight. **145** lbs. Chest : Res **33-3/4** inches ; inspiration **35-3/8** inches ; expiration **32½** inches. Abdomen **30½** inches.

14. Cardiovascular system : Heart **Negative**
    Blood pressure : S.. **122** ..., D.. **74** ..,Pulse : Rate—Sitting **100** ....Immediately after exercise. **106**
    Two Minutes after exercise.... **98** ...... Character....
    Arteries.... **Normal** .... Varicose veins...... **None**

15. Respiratory system...... **Negative**
16. X-ray of chest⁵...... **Negative**
17. Skin and lymphatics.... **Negative** ....Endocrine system .... **Negative**
18. Bones, joints, and muscles .. **Negative** ....Feet .. **Negative**
19. Abdominal viscera .. .. **Negative**
20. Hernia .. .. **Negative** .... Hemorrhoids .... **None**

1 Appointment, promotion, retirement, annual, active duty, special.
2 Regular Army ; National Guard ; Officers' Reserve Corps ; Reserve Officer's Training Corps.
3 If annual physical examination, record only for past year.
4 If annual physical examination, record only distant and near vision, and state whether defect is properly corrected.
5 When indicated.
6 Not required for annual physical examination.
7 If rejected for appointment in Regular Army because of malocclusion, send plaster models to the Surgeon General.
8 Required for candidates for commission.

D., A. G. O. Form No. 63
(August 1, 1939)

21. Genito urinary system .... Negative ....
22. Nervous system .... Negative ....
23. Laboratory procedures : Kahn¹ .... Negative .... Wassermann¹ ....
    Urinalysis : Sp. gr. .... 1.022 .... Albumin Negative .... Sugar .... Negative ....
    Microscopical (if indicated)¹ .... Negative ....
    Other laboratory procedures ....
24. Remarks on defects not sufficiently described ....
    .... This Officer was imprisoned for over 2 years, made a good adjustment to it -
    is now a bit apathetic, but mildly so. He shows no psychiatric disorder,
    .... IMPRESSION: Class B, Non-patient
    .... /s/ DONALD B. PETERSON
    .... Lt Colonel, MC
    ....

25. Corrective measures, or other action recommended ....
    ....

26. Is the individual permanently incapacitated for active service ? ....
    If yes, specify defect ....

27. If applicant for appointment : Does he meet physical requirements ? .... Do you recommend acceptance with
    minor physical defects ? .... If rejection is recommended, specify cause ....

28. Examinee states he is .... drawing a pension, disability allowance, or compensation or retired pay from the U. S.
    Government. If yes, state disability ....

    .... JAMES S. PEGG, ... Colonel, Dental   Corps
                                    (Name and grade)

.... 142D GENERAL HOSPITAL, APO 465 ...
        (Place)   GEORGE W. PRICE, ... Major, Medical   Corps.
                                                    (Name and grade)

        17   May   1.45
            (Date)   ROBERT G. HYAMS, .. Captain, Medical   Corps.
                                                    (Name and grade)

                            1st Ind.

Headquarters ....
To the Commanding General ....
Remarks and recommendations ....
....

                        ....
                                            (Name)

            ....
                (Grade)   (Organization and arm or service)
                                                                    Commanding.

                        2nd Ind.,

...., 19 .... To The Adjutant General.
....
....
....

1. Required for candidates for commission.
2. State action taken on recommendations of the board. If incapacitated for active service, state whether action by retiring board is
   recommended.

HEADQUARTERS U.S. AIR FORCES IN INDIA
TENTH U.S. AIR FORCE

New Delhi, India,
July 15, 1942.

GENERAL ORDERS)
:
NUMBER   16)

EXTRACT

Under provisions of AR 600-45, the following officers
and enlisted men are awarded the Silver Star for exceptional
gallantry in the face of enemy aerial activity:

*   *   *   *   *

2nd Lt. KENNETH F. HORNER, 0435393, Navigator.

*   *   *   *   *

These officers and men, did, on or about June 4th,
1942, participate in a mission over Lower Burma in a B-17 E.
Their assigned mission to bomb shipping and docks in the Rangoon
area was accomplished through extremely adverse weather
conditions, which necessitated very low flying, and for the
greater part was carried out under heavy attack from enemy
fighters and severe anti-aircraft fire. In returning they
met with enemy fighter resistance of over twenty aircraft.
During this running fight they destroyed at least four enemy
planes before having the right rudder control and two engines
disabled, and the tail and side gunners put out of action,
nevertheless, they continued to fight their way through.

In this engagement, which ultimately required the
forced landing of the plane, after all but the pilot and
co-pilot had parachuted, four members of the crew were
wounded and one was killed.

This personnel has, in these accomplishments, and
in the forced landing of the plane under such difficult
mechanical conditions, exhibited outstanding courage, coolness,
quick and precise decision in action, and gallantry of the
highest order.

A TRUE EXTRACT COPY:

WILLIAM L. VAN VLECK,
Major, Air Corps.

/s/ Earl L. Naiden,
/t/ EARL L. NAIDEN
Brigadier General, U.S.A.,
Commanding.

The Silver Star Medal is the third highest military decoration for valor that can be awarded to any person serving in the United States Armed Forces.

The medal is awarded for gallantry in action against an enemy of the United States.

The gallantry displayed must have taken place while in action against an enemy of the United States, while engaged in military operations involving conflict with an opposing foreign force, or while serving with friendly foreign forces engaged in an armed conflict against an opposing armed force in which the United States is not a belligerent party.

It was first awarded in 1932, the Silver Star medal is the successor award to the Citation Star which was established by an Act of Congress on July 8, 1918.

14 May 1945

Subject: Transfer to Office of Strategic Services

To: Commanding Officer
    OSS Detachment 101
    APO 629, c/o P. M., New York

1.   It is requested that I be transferred to the Office of Strategic Services, China Theater.

2.   The following personal data is furnished:

    Name: Kenneth Foster Horner
    Rank: 1st Lt. (13 May 1945)
    Serial Number: O-435393
    Branch: Air Corps
    Assignment: Navigator (B-17)
    Military Service: Commissioned 2nd Lt.
      10 February 1941; assigned to 88th Reconnaissance Squadron; prisoner of war from 4 June 1942 until 29 April 1945.

    Present Address: Detachment Patients, Ward 54
        142 General Hospital, APO 465

3.   The medical examination at the 142 General Hospital indicates that I am in good physical condition and that there is nothing to prevent my returning to active duty. I have previously indicated my desire to return to combat, but I am willing to accept any assignment given me for which I am qualified. I do not want to return to the United States until such time as the war in China is successfully completed.

Kenneth Foster Horner
Kenneth Foster Horner
1st Lt., AC

MIA: Missing In Action   173

BASIC: Ltr fr 1st Lt Kenneth F. Horner to CO, OSSSU Det 101,
        APO 629, Subj: "Transfer to OSS" dtd 14 May 1945.

201. Horner, Kenneth F. (Off)   1st Ind   WRP/mfs

OFFICE OF THE COMMANDING OFFICER, OSSSU DET 101, APO 629, 18 May 45.

TO: Headquarters, USF, India-Burma Theater, APO 885.

    1. If the request contained in basic communication does
not violate any of the Theater policies regarding reassignment
of former Prisoners of War, request favorable consideration of
this application.

    2. OSS, China Theater, has sufficient slots in its T.O.
to cover transfer of this officer to that organization. (See
attached letter giving authority to recruit personnel for filling
vacancies in TO of OSS, China Theater.

                        W. R. PEERS
                        Colonel, INF.
                        Commanding

201-Horner, Kenneth F.(O)(14 May 45)   2nd Ind.   EJM/sg
7
HEADQUARTERS, UNITED STATES FORCES, INDIA BURMA THEATER, APO 885,
26 May 1945.

TO: Commanding Officer, O.S.S.S.U. Detachment 101, APO 629.

     Not favorably considered.
     BY COMMAND OF LIEUTENANT GENERAL SULTAN:

                        E. J. MCENTEE,
                        Capt., A.G.D.,
                        Asst. Adj. Gen.

BASIC: Ltr fr 1st Lt. Kenneth F. Horner, to CO,OSSSU Det 101,
APO 689, Subj: "Transfer to OSS" dtd 14 May 1945.

201-Horner,Kenneth F. (Off)   3rd Ind   WRP/mfs
(14 May 45)
OFFICE OF THE COMMANDING OFFICER,OSSSU DET 101, APO 689, 5 June 45.

TO: 1st Lt Kenneth F. Horner, Detachment of Patients, Ward 54,
142 General Hospital, APO 465.

     1. The subject of your transfer and the transfer of Lt.
Humphries to Detachment 101 was discussed personally with the
Theater Commander. Your request was not looked upon with favor,
primarily due to a recent WD publication covering the assignment
of personnel in your category.

     2. It is regretable this situation does exist, as we would
have definitely desired your services. Would you kindly notify
Lt. Humphries of contents of Paragraph 2, above?

                              W. R. PEERS
                              Colonel, INF.
                              Commanding

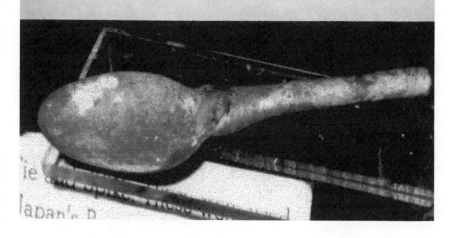

I made this spoon for E. Sydney Quick. After his
death, his wife Rose gave his prison memorabilia to the
Admiral Nimitz Museum in Fredericksburg, Texas.

OFFICE OF THE THEATER FISCAL DIRECTOR
UNITED STATES FORCES
INDIA   BURMA

JOS/srg
APO 885

19 February 1946

SUBJECT: Claim by Maung Tun Myaing

THRU: The Adjutant General, War Department, Washington 25, D. C.

TO: 1st Lt. Kenneth F. Horner, 0-435393

· This office is in receipt of a claim presented by the Senior
Civil Affairs Officer (British) Pegu, Burma on behalf of Maung Tun
Myaing of Naungpattaya, Waw Township, for his services rendered to E.P.
and BORs. The claim is supported by a written statement as follows:

"(Name in Burmese)

TO: United States Army Paymaster General.

        Pay to above Rs 1200 for services rendered to
E.P. and BORS (formerly POWs) and deduct same from the
pay of

                        2nd Lt. K. F. Horner
                        0-435393
                        216 North Lopez Street
                        New Orleans, La.

                /s/ Kenneth F. Horner."

        It is requested that this office be advised as to whether or not
this Rs 1200 ($363.15) has been deducted from your pay. If such ded-
uction WXXXWXWEXXWXWXIXXWEXXWWXXWXWXXWXXWXIIWXIX has been made. a
complete citation to the voucher on which deduction was made, should
be furnished this office including name of disbursing officer, voucher
number, and month of accounts.

        Any further information you may be able to furnish regarding the
circumstances of this claim should be forwarded.

        FOR THE THEATER FISCAL DIRECTOR:

                        JAMES O. SMITH
                        Captain, FD
                        Assistant

Parents Get Cablegram from Son After Three Years Without Word

For almost three years Mr. and Mrs. B. H. Horner, 216 North Lopez street, had no word of their son except that he was missing. Wednesday came a cablegram from First Lieutenant Kenneth F. Horner saying "I'm well and fit."

He had been liberated April 29 by retreating Japanese forces in Burma and, according to a New York Times story by Tillman Durain, Sergeant Tyman H. Wells, Jr., Hattiesburg, Miss., was also freed then. Lieutenant Horner's message, which followed the war department notification of his liberation, said he was in the hospital and "hope to see you soon."

The Horners had been pinning their faith since June 4, 1942, on the words of their son's pilot—"There's a fifty-fifty chance he got through." Mrs. Horner was too happy and excited to retell the story more than sketchily, but apparently the AAF plane on which her son was an aerial navigator was damaged, the crew bailed out

and the pilot and copilot made a try at getting back to their base, and did. Their son, who is 26 years old, had never been reported a prisoner of war.

Correspondent Durain's story tells of 429 "emaciated, hungry, ragged American and British former prisoners of war, who were set free by the retreating Japanese at the end of three nights of forced marching from Rangoon" to near Pegu, Burma. Most of the men marched barefooted, he said. An American major, dressed as a Burmese and led by two friendly Burmese, made his way through groups of Japanese to British headquarters, which rushed trucks to pick up the liberated men.

"Air Corps men, American and British, received especially brutal treatment," Durain wrote. "Most were confined in dark cells for the first several months of captivity. The Japanese said Air Corps men were criminals."

Enlargement of article shown at right

My parents and I resumed life as if I had never been missing. Of course, my homecoming was more than any of us dared to dream during my time away. We never discussed my prison experiences.

Sadly, my father died just a short three years later at the young age of 56. I moved my mother and sister to Tampa.

My mother lived a full life of 86 years, but never remarried.

Jeanne Odile and Benjamin Harrison Horner, my folks.

Missing 3 Years, N. O. Officer Is Alive

awarded the Silver Star, Mr. and Mrs. Horner understand. He was one of the first Army airmen sent to the Indian theatre.

Before entering service, he was with the Freeport Sulphur Co. here.

Men Of The Sou

OFFICIAL PUBLICATION OF THE ALUMNI ASSOCIATION OF LOYOLA UN

Vol. X   NEW ORLEANS, JUNE, 1945

MAY, 1945

BACK HON

LT. HORNER
... he's safe ...

By Marjorie H. Roehl

For almost three years the family of First Lt. Kenneth E. Horner hoped and prayed. This week their burden of worry was lifted.

Lt. Horner, who had been listed as missing in action since June, 1942, is "well, fit, in the hospital and hope to see you soon." The message from him has just come to his overjoyed family.

The lieutenant, 216 N. Lopez St., was one of several hundred American prisoners rescued from a Jap prison camp in Rangoon, Burma. He had never been listed as a prisoner of war. Japs attacked the B-17 Flying Fortress on which Lt. Horner was navigator, way back in 1942. He bailed out.

Now his parents, Mr. and Mrs. B. H. Horner, are only waiting for his return. The lieutenant, along with the rest of his crew, has been

Lieut. Kenneth F. Horner, Assoc., who was in a Japanese prison camp for two years and eleven months, during which time he lost 80 pounds, was recently rescued from Rangoon and arrived in New Orleans late in June.

Horner Freed After 3 Years In Jap Prison

After almost three years with no word of their son except that he was "missing," the parents of Lieut. Kenneth F. Horner, Assoc., received notice early in May that he was a prisoner of the Japanese and a few days later had a cablegram from him saying, "I'm well and fit." He had been liberated on April 29 by retreating Japanese forces in Burma and was in a hospital, but added: "I hope to see you soon."

On June 4, 1942, Lieut. Horner's parents were told by his pilot "there's a 50-50 chance he got through" after the plane on which he was an aerial navigator was damaged. The crew bailed out and the pilot and co-pilot made a try at getting back to their base—and did.

Emaciated, Hungry

A story in the New York Times by Tillman Durain tells of 429 "emaciated, hungry, ragged American and British former prisoners of war who were set free by the retreating Japanese at the end of three nights of forced marching from Rangoon" to near Pegu, Burma. Most of the men marched barefooted, he said.

The newspaper account of the liberation of the party added that an American major, dressed as a Burmese and led by two friendly Burmese, made his way through groups of Japanese to British headquarters, which rushed trucks to pick up the liberated men. "Air Corps men, American and British, received especially brutal treatment," Durain wrote. "Most were confined in dark cells for the first several months of captivity. The Japanese said Air Corps men were ...

Missing Three Years, Lt. K. Horner Is Alive

LT. HORNER
he's safe

For almost three years the parents of 1st Lt. Kenneth E. Horner, 216 N. Lopez Street, hoped and prayed. On May 4th their prayer was answered and their burden of worry over.

Lt. Horner who had been listed as missing in action since June of '42, is "safe, still alive and well in a hospital in India and hopes to see all soon." He cabled his overjoyed mother on May 15th.

The 27-year-old lieutenant was one of the several hundred American prisoners rescued from a Jap prison camp in Rangoon, Burma, both by the American and British Forces on April 29th. Lt. Horner had never been listed as a prisoner of war. The Japs attacked the B-17 Flying Fortress on which Kenneth Horner was a navigator, back in June, 1942. He bailed out and was picked up by the Japs. The pilot and co-pilot of the AAF plane got back to their base.

Mr. and Mrs. B. H. Horner, the happiest parents in New Orleans, are eagerly waiting for the return of their long missing son. Kenneth with the rest of his crew has been awarded the Silver Star. He was the first of the Army Airmen to be sent into the India theatre.

Before entering the service back in February, 1941, Kenneth Horner was a graduate of Warren Easton and finished at Loyola. Later he was employed by the Freeport Sulphur Co.

Lieut. KENNE
NER, Assoc., free
anese prison can
dia, in a non-com
ity and then retu
New Orleans. Pr
lease his family
word from him fo
years. He was at
gator.

I was honored to have been presented with the "Key to the City" of New Orleans upon my return home.

Ariel view of abandoned Rangoon Prison, liberation 1945

As stated in Wikipedia ® the prison is still in use today under the name of "Insein Prison". It is run by the

2013 Google Maps ®

military Junta of Myanmar, the State Peace and Development Council, and is largely used to repress political dissidents.

One of its most famous prisoners is the Nobel Peace Prize winning human rights activist, Aung San Suu Kyi, who has been confined to Insein on three separate occasions in 2003, 2007 and 2009.

Typical Cell Block - Rangoon Prison

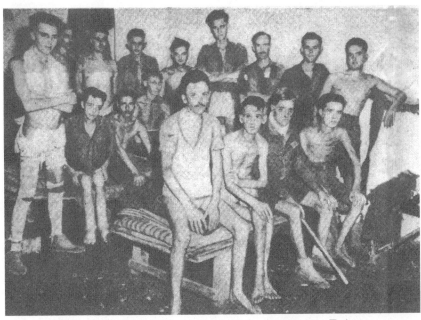

Men liberated from hospital - Rangoon Prison

Lt. George Wilson

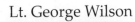

M.Sgt. Fletcher Hart

BY SKILLFUL MANIPULATION AND SHEER COURAGE, MAJOR FRANK D. SHARP, THE PILOT AND COPILOT LT. H.E. WUNDERLICH KEPT THE CRIPPLED SHIP IN THE AIR UNTIL THEY SIGHTED A BRITISH-HELD VILLAGE NEAR WHICH THEY CRASH-LANDED....

ALTHOUGH WRECKED, THE FORTRESS DID NOT FALL INTO ENEMY HANDS... SOMEWHAT SHAKEN UP, BUT OTHERWISE UNHURT, THE TWO AMERICAN FLYERS CAREFULLY DESTROYED THE PRECIOUS BOMB-SIGHT WITH RIFLE BULLETS...

LEAVING THEIR ILL-FATED BOMBER TO BE SALVAGED BY THE BRITISH, IF POSSIBLE, THE BRAVE AMERICANS FOUGHT THEIR WAY THROUGH THE JUNGLE BACK TO INDIA...

NEARLY A MONTH LATER, JULY 2ND, MAJ. SHARP AND LT. WUNDERLICH ARRIVED IN CALCUTTA WHERE THEY MADE THEIR REPORT. ONE OF THE CREW DEAD, SIX BELIEVED TO BE PRISONERS... ON AUG. 20TH, THE WAR DEPARTMENT AWARDED THE "SILVER STAR" FOR EXCEPTIONAL GALLANTRY TO THE NINE-MAN CREW OF THAT FLYING FORTRESS!

THE ARMY "SILVER STAR" IS AWARDED TO DESERVING SOLDIERS OF THE U.S. ARMY IN TIME OF WAR FOR GALLANTRY IN ACTION IN SITUATIONS NOT WARRANTING THE AWARD OF EITHER THE ARMY MEDAL OF HONOR OR THE ARMY DISTINGUISHED SERVICE CROSS...

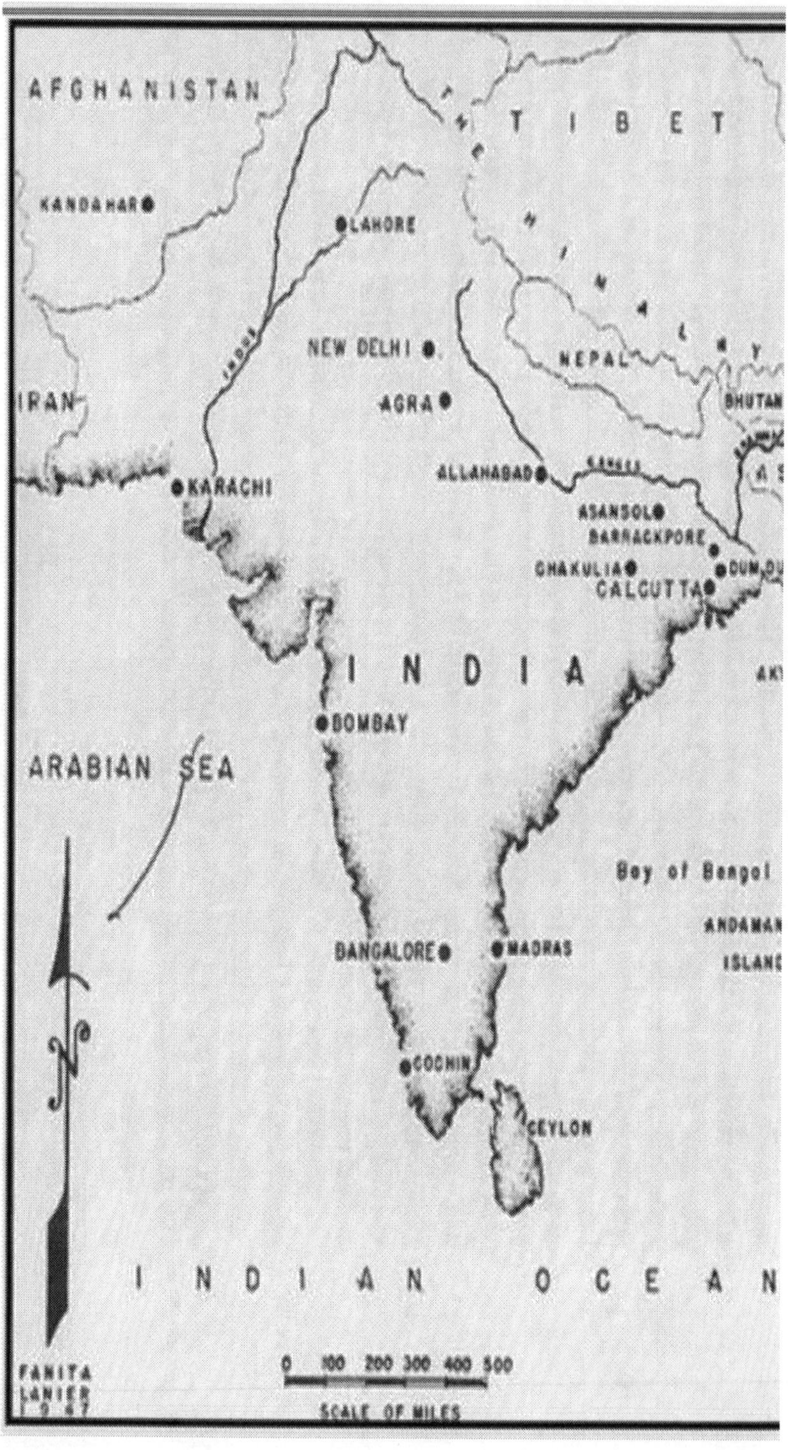

AFGHANISTAN

TIBET

KANDAHAR●

●LAHORE

NEW DELHI ●

NEPAL

IRAN

AGRA ●

BHUTAN

KARACHI●

ALLAHABAD●

ASANSOL●
BARRACKPORE●
CHAKULIA●
CALCUTTA●
DUM DUM

I N D I A

AKY

●BOMBAY

ARABIAN SEA

Bay of Bengal

ANDAMAN
ISLAND

BANGALORE●

●MADRAS

●COCHIN

CEYLON

I N D I A N   O C E A N

FANITA
LANIER
1947

0   100   200   300   400   500

SCALE OF MILES

Kenneth Horner, "Jack", lives in
Tampa, Florida with his wife and
daughter. MIA is his first
published work.

He is available to answer any questions
concerning the China Burma India Theatre of
Operation in WWII or his personal experience.

If interested in communicating
with him please do so at:
hornerkf@gmail.com

Cover design and photograph above
by his daughter Connie

31987652R00119

Made in the USA
Charleston, SC
04 August 2014